On the Doorposts of All Our Houses

(and what went on inside)

Donna Siegel

iUniverse, Inc.
New York Bloomington

On the Doorposts of All Our Houses
(and what went on inside)

iUniverse books may be ordered through booksellers or by contacting:

iUniverse
1663 Liberty Drive
Bloomington, IN 47403
www.iuniverse.com
1-800-Authors (1-800-288-4677)

ISBN: 978-1-4502-5948-4 (pbk)
ISBN: 978-1-4502-5949-1 (ebk)

Printed in the United States of America

iUniverse rev. date: 10/15/2010

For everyone mentioned in this book,
living or dead (especially them) …

"If you don't believe in ghosts,
you've never been to a family reunion."
—Ashleigh Brilliant

Contents

Top l to r: Hodel, Mayer Schulman; George, Anne Schulman
Middle: Max, Jacob, Ray Simon; Sarah (Bobo) Simon; Ike Babbitt
Bottom: Harry, Elsie, Helen, Mayer, Hodel, Lillian, George

we were fruitful and we multiplied
Top row: Vicki Gammill, Ron Schulman, Anne Schulman, George Schulman
2nd row: Larry Gammill, Linda Schulman, Paul/Rick Schulman, Donna Siegel
3rd row: Ashely Siegel, Rebecca Schulman, Phil Flowers
4th row: Jane Stein, Michael Stein, Lori Siegel, Jon Siegel
5th row: Elliot Stein, Nathan Stein, Alexis Siegel
Cats, Howard and Simon Schulman; Yellow Lab, Maggie Gamill; Great Dane, Griffin Siegel; Schnauzer, Baxter Flowers; Labradoodle, Harley Stein; Maltese, Emmy and Oscar Siegel

top, l to r: Oz, Siegels, Greenswags, Davises; Natalie Harris, my wedding; Charlie's, Siegels, Greenswags, Davises.
2nd row: Pat Kaufman, Grace Salamonovitz, Ruth Brodsky, Jean Goldberg; Linda Friedman, me; Harriette Freeman, me, in Russia.
3rd row: Helen and Sammy Simkin, me; upper gold frame, Lois Landa; lower frame, Louise Siegel; upper far right group, Norma Brecher, me, Jeannie Davis, Louise Greenswag; lower far right group, me, Kay Bucksbaum, Louise Greenswag.
bottom: Betty Freundlich, Jean Goldberg, Iris Siegel, Pat Kaufman, Ruth Brodsky.

Preface: In Lieu of a Gravestone

"I've given my memoirs far more
thought than any of my marriages.
You can't divorce a book."
—Gloria Swanson

This book began as a pushy, unwelcome thought. It launched its attack as I stood near my father's newly engraved headstone in a cemetery in Omaha, Nebraska. Next to his grave was my mother's—with its matching headstone. Tidy rows of similar granite headstones belonging to my grandparents and other deceased family surrounded them.

Gazing at this homogeneous scene, I remember thinking, "They are as connected in death as they were in life." Then I realized this would be the last generation of our family to be buried together. We had become "nuclear." This certain dispersion of our family was disturbing.

In the cemetery with me that day were my brothers, Ron and Rick, my sister, Vicki, my daughter, Jane, and the few remaining members of our family still living in Omaha—destined to take their places among the grassy mounds we contemplated.

We had been mute and respectful at first, but as our stories about the deceased grew livelier and more irreverent, our incongruous laughter floated over the scene as if a runaway soundtrack had lurched into what should have been a silent movie.

The irreverence served to resuscitate our loved ones, however briefly. I knew only death could prevent the noisy protests of those occupants in the tidy rows from chiming in, "No, no, that's not the way it happened." I knew this because few stories made it to the punch line unchallenged when they were alive.

Jane interrupted my reverie. "If you're going to be cremated, where will I visit you?" With this question, the unsolicited thought flickered to life. On an internal screen, I could see the coming attractions of that one-sided visit (such as we were having now), with me speechless and unable to utter, "No, no, that's not the way it happened." The unbidden thought intensified as the internal screen suddenly produced a narrator: "Why not avoid all this by leaving behind a book of family stories?" That thought cruised along on automatic pilot for a few months until it engendered enough power to take on an even more intrusive life of its own.

"Not living on in anyone's memory makes death even

more tragic, don't you think?" the internal narrator oozed one day. "And what about those immigrants whose bravery saved your family from the death camps? Shouldn't they be remembered—if not in deathless prose, at least in yours?" What chutzpah! Who died and made this figment of my imagination a literary critic?

I may have heard the faint strains of a stirring march by John Philip Sousa as the narrator persisted, "And what about the sacrifices of the next generation? Didn't they enable your generation to achieve the American Dream?" There was a brief, very pregnant pause. "Not to mention all the generations to come—bereft, robbed of a written heritage." That was the clincher: those disenfranchised future generations who would never know us.

Although the seed for this book was planted that day in Omaha, who could have guessed it would have such a long gestation? During this interval, the whole immigrant generation of our family died, and a lusty new generation was born and firmly established itself: my niece, Rebecca, and my three grandchildren, Alexis, Nathan, and Elliot. Finally, at the age of seventy-nine, I am delivering this book.

Writing it permitted me to relive those precious days and provided a few unexpected epiphanies along the way. I offer this story as an account of one family's journey from the Polish and Russian *shtetls*—the settlements where Eastern European Jews were forced to live—to our assimilated, wireless lives of today. Similar stories echo through countless other families from a multitude of other countries.

In the struggle to provide a better life, much has been gained. Still, remembering the occupants of that cemetery and the legacy they bequeathed, I wonder if something precious was inadvertently lost.

I hope this memoir will serve as a place where my children and grandchildren can visit me. Perhaps they will gain a broader and deeper sense of their own history, even discover something about themselves here.

Of course, writing this book has given me an uncontested, unchallenged chance to say, "This is the way it happened."

Introduction: The Chambered Nautilus and Me

"One person's introduction is another person's chapter one."
—Author Unknown

The chambered nautilus, eloquently described by Oliver Wendell Holmes as "a ship of pearl," produces a bigger home as it grows and carries all the outgrown ones with it through its life. I appear doomed to the same fate.

In the process of writing this book, I discovered that I am not only carrying around all the houses I write about here, but with the tenacity of kudzu, they have entwined themselves around my memories and usurped this memoir. In resurrecting these sets, it seems I have also exhumed the characters of my life who were just waiting for the curtain to rise to resume their earlier dramas. All I had to do was watch and record the action.

Here I am, for example, observing myself as a child of six or seven, in Sioux City, Iowa, elbows on the white tablecloth that covers my grandparents' dining room table, listening to the grownups talk while they drink tea in glasses (spoons still in them). In the center of the table is the perpetual still life of prayer books and candlesticks at the ready to usher in our next meal. In soft focus, barely visible in the background, is the worn upright piano. I don't have to see the keyboard to know that most of the keys have lost their faux-ivory coats and now resemble small brown oars; I can still hear the throbbing sounds they made, wobbling like Jell-O through the air as I struck them.

But now the scene has changed. I am in Iowa City, a freshman at the University of Iowa. I am lying on my bunk in one of many hastily erected Quonset huts built on the banks of the Iowa River to accommodate the school's burgeoning enrollment, which now includes servicemen returning from World War II.

It is spring 1949. Behind my bunk are snapshots hanging from tacks on a bulletin board. I am surrounded by books assigned in the liberal arts classes that my Uncle Ray says I should take because they will make me a well-rounded wife capable of interesting dinner table conversation. I have never thought about a career, and no one has ever suggested that I have one; in fact, I am the first woman in my family to go to college. As electives, I have taken philosophy and modern literature.

Fast forward again, and I am in Davenport, Iowa, a leafy river town that snakes along the shore of the Mississippi just sixty miles from Iowa City. I am presiding over one of those dinner parties for which I have been so carefully groomed. Soft golden light illuminates the dining room in the house my former husband and I have built here in Davenport, where his family's jewelry store is located. On the buffet is a charming French clock flanked by two brass altarpieces, which we bought as a set at an antique show (without dickering). Sitting around the carefully appointed table are several of our friends, probably eight of them—just the right number for interesting conversations and as far as the table can expand comfortably.

The scene changes once more. I am sitting at the same dining room table, but now I am alone in Santa Barbara, California. Books again surround me, but these books are technical and wouldn't lead to interesting dinner table conversations—unless the guests happen to be interested in the physics of light or additive color theory. The soft glow is gone; it has been replaced by harsh sunlight streaming through louvered windows onto a Mexican tile floor. A patio with tropical plants and climbing bougainvillea lies just beyond.

Most of the places I'm still carrying around with me vanished from the planet long ago. I now live on the eighteenth floor of a high-rise condominium in Houston, Texas, where this book was written. More precisely, it was written in a walk-in closet I have transformed into my "office."

My life here represents an attempt to live as urbane and unencumbered an existence as possible at my age. It offers the benefits (and the deductions) of home ownership without the detritus of lawnmowers, country kitchens, or family rooms with functional areas. If I ever hungered to own the latest or the biggest of anything, that craving has long passed.

Yet, despite the cartons of possessions I have given or thrown away in the interest of living this streamlined life (imagine white ceramic floors, neutral walls, and mostly bare bay windows), my overstuffed past seems to have pervaded this nest as it has all the others. It's the nautilus syndrome, an opportunistic disease against which I seem to have no immunity.

Amid the glass, leather, and stainless steel are ornate gifts commemorating milestone events, some of which I no longer remember. One of those brass altarpieces still sits on the buffet. The other one has been replaced by a large ceramic egg through which four long-necked giraffes appear to be emerging, bought in Mexico on the last trip I took with my Davenport friends—friendships that have endured for sixty years.

On the wall near the couch, mounted in an antique frame, is the small bronze figure I found years ago at a giant garage sale in Rome. In the guest bedroom hangs a painting of the bridge that connects Davenport and Moline, Illinois. My friend Harriette, who died last year, painted it for me when I left Iowa to begin a new life.

Most of my furniture, still looking good though upholstered again and again, goes back to the early days of my marriage. My books, on shelves and in stacks, reveal the progression of my eclectic life: *Statistics and Applications to the Biological and Health Sciences,* Remington and Schork; *Art, Mind and Brain,* Howard Gardner; *How You Can Make $25,000 a Year Writing (No Matter Where You Live),* Nancy Edmonds Hanson; *The Dancing Wu Li Masters,* Gary Zukav; *The Jewish Book of Why,* Alfred Kolatch; and *Si Nous Ecrivions,* my tattered but beloved high school French book.

In a kitchen drawer is my grandmother's worn brass spoon from Russia. My grandfather's *havdalah* spice holder—used to signify the end of the Sabbath and still smelling of cloves and allspice—sits on the hunt table in the living room. Odd serving pieces from my mother's sterling silverware, wrapped in Pacific cloth, live in a drawer in my buffet. The bottom drawer of the breakfront holds my father's *tallis* (prayer shawl), his *tefillin* (small prayer boxes attached to leather strips, which are called phylacteries), and the big blue box of pictures I may never get around to pasting into albums. And so it goes.

The stories that follow will meander through other houses and other rooms, where the characters in the story are waiting.

The House on Lake Street

"I could make my grandmother happy just by being hungry."
—Jean-Paul Sartre

Arguments over nature or nurture are a moot point when you grow up in a Jewish immigrant family. In these families, nature and nurture are inextricable: a seamless blend, just one big *tzimmes.* If you are unfamiliar with the word, you can apply either of its definitions: a stew of various ingredients, or a state of confusion. In my case, it also became the core around which my identity wrapped itself.

All four of my grandparents emigrated from Europe, my mother's family from Poland, my father's from Russia. Life in the shtetls was difficult—think *Fiddler on the Roof* without Zero Mostel and all the singing and dancing. Despite the hardships, my grandparents assumed they would live and die there. They were already married to appropriate mates who had been selected for them; they had children and a village full of family and friends.

But with the onslaught of civil war and certain conscription, their already precarious lives deteriorated rapidly. Ghetto life, with its daily humiliations, was one thing, but dying on behalf of an inhospitable country that considered Jews second-class citizens was too much to ask.

With nothing more substantial than the dream of providing a better life for their families, my grandfathers bravely left their wives and children and joined the flood of immigrants flowing into this country around the time of World War I. Each of my grandfathers arrived alone, nearly penniless, and unable to speak or understand English.

Since both of my grandfathers entered this country through the port of Galveston, Texas, I have wondered if they happened to be there at the same time—perhaps sitting on the same bench as they waited to appear before the official who would determine their fates (and their new surnames), never dreaming how fate would unite them later in their lives. But I will never know because exact dates have long been forgotten.

Although my grandfathers had been scholars in Europe, they took menial work here to earn the passage to bring their families over. This process took many years, but neither they nor their abandoned families ever lost hope. (This is beginning to sound like a movie; in fact, I think I've seen it in many languages, with subtitles.)

As a child listening to the chilling stories about the dangers they managed to overcome, I admired their courage, but it was hard to think of them as heroes. Neither resembled the heroic figures I was familiar with: King Edward, Charles Lindbergh, and Franklin Delano Roosevelt. With their broken English and foreign ways, they seemed to knew less about the world than I did; yet they had been brave enough to travel across countries—even continents. And they had crossed the ocean to America, like Columbus, while I had never ventured beyond my neighborhood.

While my grandfathers were working in the United States, my grandmothers struggled to make a living for themselves and their children. Neither of them had any special education or training, but they were both highly skilled when it came to survival. Stretching a *kopeck* was a way of life in the shtetl, something you inherited along with the family prayer books, silver candlesticks, and an unquestioned reverence for the old traditions.

As for sacrificing the present for the future, the Little Red Hen was an amateur compared to my grandmothers. To them, the present was just a prelude to the main event. They both lived their whole lives preparing for tomorrow. While they waited for the passage money to arrive, my father's mother ran a small general merchandise store that belonged to her family, in the town of Petrikov (which I'm pretty sure still exists); my mother's mother, from a poorer family, developed her latent entrepreneurial skills by smuggling cigarettes across the border to sell to the Russian soldiers.

When the families were reunited at last, my grandmothers marveled at their modern conveniences, but they resolutely followed their time-honored traditions. They continued to keep kosher homes and to preserve their strong Jewish identities, passing along their convictions—

if not all their practices—to the next generation: my parents and their siblings.

My mother's family settled in Omaha, Nebraska, and my father's family settled in Sioux City, Iowa. Although they lived just sixty miles apart, they met for the first time many years later, following what seemed to me to be another perilous act of bravery: my parents' elopement. This astonishing and uncharacteristic act took place after a very short courtship, and the ceremony was not performed by a rabbi, but by a *goyishe* (gentile) justice of the peace.

I'm not sure which of their transgressions—the elopement or being married by a gentile justice of the peace—produced the most hand wringing by the two families, but it was mutually decided that since the damage was done, the proper authorities should bless this union. A religious ceremony followed two weeks later.

This presented us with a dilemma: Which date should be celebrated? I'm not sure why the Jewish one was chosen, but it gave my siblings and me two extra weeks to think up an appropriate anniversary gift. As it happened, we could never to come up with anything they actually wanted anyway.

Although we visited both sets of grandparents several times a year, in the early days we spent more time in Omaha. I loved the rambling wooden house on Lake Street where my mother's parents, Jacob and Sarah Simon, lived with my two unmarried uncles, Max and Ray, and an endless procession of cats.

My relationship with Ray is complicated. He was my

uncle, but he was only eight years older than I, having been born after my grandparents were reunited in this country. This put him in the awkward position of straddling two generations when it came to me: sometimes he was a playmate, sometimes he was a big brother, and sometimes he was a babysitter (particularly for the Saturday matinee cliffhanger).

He was also a full-time source of miscellaneous information, some of which came directly, but some by stealth—I spied on him whenever I could. Most of the time, it wasn't that interesting, but once, as I watched through the keyhole in the kitchen door, I caught him playing strip poker with his boy friends. I told him about it to make him nervous, but I never really saw anything.

Ray was going on thirteen and I was going on five the year my mother and I lived with them all in the Lake Street house. My siblings were not yet born, and my father did not live with us that year; my mother said it was because he was working in Chicago. I accepted her explanation without question. Besides, there were plenty of adults to take his place. Most of them came and went every day, but my grandmother was always there to take care of me.

I was the center of the universe—an exalted position I held until Ron, my first sibling, appeared and ruined everything. By then, though, my mother and I weren't living in the Lake Street house anymore and everything had changed.

According to pictures, I was a skinny kid with knobby knees and braids tied at the ends with rubber bands or string. It's amazing how oblivious you can be at that age about the major events taking place around you. I thought everyone was as happy as I was. I had my two cats, Wallis Simpson and King Edward, always waiting for me in the backyard, ready to rub their furry bodies against my legs and lick my fingers with their sandpaper tongues.

And I was free to roam the entire house unsupervised from the cellar to the attic, except for the small back bedroom near the kitchen, which was occupied by a mysterious parade of shadowy strangers, sometimes called "the roomer" and sometimes "the boarder." These men were indistinguishable from each other (at least to me). They appeared at breakfast and dinner to be fed by my grandmother, after which they silently disappeared, either into their room or out of the house, presumably to go to their jobs. The door to that room was always closed; perhaps it was even locked.

With so much to explore, I wasn't even curious about it. Equipped with a first-born child's vivid imagination, I wandered through the house every day making up adventures. My explorations began in the cellar if Bobo, my grandmother, happened to be working in her kitchen. ("Bobo" was my early attempt to say *bubbe,* the Yiddish word for grandmother. Even after I could say it, I continued to call her Bobo. After a while, the whole family called her Bobo, and it became her name for the rest of her life.)

I liked to know she was in the kitchen when I went down to the cellar, because it was scary down there. I had to leave the warm shelter of the kitchen, walk past Bobo's sewing machine in the back hall, and descend the rickety wooden stairs to the damp, musty domain of the "boogeyman," an invisible menace that stalked this lower region, according to my Uncle Ray. Although I had never seen him, I could feel his dark, hooded presence watching me.

To make sure I didn't catch a glimpse of him—after which it would be too scary to go down there alone ever again—I always looked straight ahead. I was willing to risk this danger because the cellar, which ran the length of the house, had amazing attractions that changed often. First of all, there was the mystery closet at the far end: Why did it have a dirt floor even though it was inside the house? How did those glass jars, with the strange objects that looked vaguely familiar, get on those shelves? I never asked. I just picked up the jars and turned them until the floating objects became a kaleidoscope of blurry shapes and colors. Then I checked the floor for worms or spiders. I ignored the worms, but if I found a spider, I poked it with my finger, spurring it to move its tiny eyelash legs.

I spent most of my time in the middle section of the cellar. I made some of my best discoveries on the shelves of the metal bookcase there; it was where discarded things ended up. Once I found a doll with a white china face. It had a lumpy cloth body and chipped china arms and legs. Traces of red paint still clung to its fingers and toes. When I picked up the doll, its eyelids opened to reveal blue glass eyes. Bobo said it had been my mother's doll. This was irrefutable evidence that my mother was once a little girl who played with dolls—even if this doll didn't look like a baby, and its stiff body felt like straw.

Another time I found a small black box with a tiny, red window. Looking into the window, I was shocked to see a face looking back at me. I reported this amazing fact to Ray as we sat on the front porch after dinner, but he just went on reading and said that I had probably seen one of the gypsies living in the box. This was even more amazing! Could there be a whole family living in that box? Whenever I was in the cellar I checked to see if the gypsies had moved out. Eventually, the box disappeared, and I forgot about it.

(Years later, I saw a box like it in a museum. A sign near it said, "Boy Scout Brownie Camera, circa 1930." A strong wave of nostalgia washed over me. I could see myself holding the box, looking for the gypsies. I could even feel the dampness of the basement and smell the dank musty air. With the memory came a sudden sense of loss. Where was that innocent little girl, so gullible that she actually believed Ray's cockamamie story? And how clever of Ray to have come up with it so quickly, not missing a beat!)

The last room in the cellar was the coal room. It had the only window in the basement, but it was interesting only on the day the coal man came. When he drove up, Bobo and I would run outside to watch him back his truck up the yard, prop open the window, and dump his load of coal through a chute right onto the floor. When winter came, Max or Ray would shovel the coal into the huge furnace that resembled a giant octopus with metal arms, which led to the registers embedded in the floors of the rooms upstairs.

The coal room was the scene of my greatest discovery. While exploring in the basement one day, I heard faint meowing sounds coming from the coal bin. Following the sound, I discovered Wally Simpson had placed her newborn kittens on top of the pile of coal. I wasn't certain they were kittens; they looked more like tiny white mice without hair.

When I ran upstairs to show one to Ray, he said my touching them made them smell like humans and Wally Simpson might not come back to feed them. Just in case, he said, we should feed them milk with a medicine dropper every day until they were big enough to crowd around a bowl and lap up the milk with their pink spoon-shaped tongues.

Although I played in the attic occasionally, I never found anything really exciting up there. Still, the boxes were overflowing with treasures I could finger endlessly: fancy clothes, high-heeled shoes, hats with beautiful feathers, and suitcases filled with books and pictures of smiling people I didn't know.

Dressed in my abandoned finery and tottering around on the high heels, I sometimes held tea parties for my paper dolls, the Princesses Margaret and Elizabeth. On these occasions, I dressed them in their best outfits and propped them up on boxes, which I decorated to resemble thrones. These tea parties were all about preparation; once everyone was dressed and the tea was poured, my interest in this ritual was over.

Before leaving the attic with my paper dolls, I always snooped through the suitcases and boxes to see if anything new had been added. Once I found some comic books my uncle Max had hidden in the bottom of one of the boxes. I didn't consider them an exciting discovery, but when I showed the comics to Bobo, I could tell she did; it was just Popeye and Olive Oyl without clothes on, but she was so upset, I decided not to tell her I had shown them to the O'Brien kids who lived across the street.

I would describe my position in my extended family that year as "favored," somewhere between "family pet" and "budding star." These were the days of Shirley Temple, a dimpled wunderkind who was the apple of every mother's eye. I think my mother was attempting to clone me (before the science even existed) into another Shirley, in case Hollywood should ever need a Jewish replacement.

Every morning, she would patiently brush my stubborn, very straight black hair around her finger into something resembling the vertical sausages so charming on blonde Shirley. Alas, with the tenacity of the desert reclaiming its aridity despite persistent irrigation—my hair quickly reverted to its straight, stringy origins, leaving me to resemble Jane Withers, another, not nearly so desirable, child star.

Despite my failure in the hair department, my mother knew she could count on me to belt out "On the Good Ship Lollypop," Shirley's and my signature song, with great enthusiasm should company drop in. If an encore were requested, I was ready with my snappy tap routine to "On the Sidewalks of New York," accompanying myself—somewhat breathlessly—by singing the lyrics: "East Side, West Side/All around the town."

For long-suffering audiences who couldn't think of a way to escape, I also knew "Shuffle Off to Buffalo." This was a far more intricate routine featuring a series of side steps followed by a quick bending of one knee to form something resembling the number four. Although the dance was supposed to be accompanied by a peppy tune, I was too busy mouthing the routine—"shuffle, hop, step"—to sing along.

Did I miss my father that year? Did I even notice he wasn't around? I don't remember. I think I just assumed that he would appear when he finished working in Chicago. More problematic, however, was the stream of gentlemen callers who came by in the evenings to see my mother. "Just friends of the family who dropped by to see all of us," she said.

Much later, when the mysteries of that year were revealed, these submerged but unforgotten memory fragments erupted, spewing out pieces of a puzzle I had kept buried in my subconscious for over forty years. Yet, for that year, Lake Street seemed as carefree as Mayberry, USA.

I did notice that Bobo never talked directly to my grandfather (*Zayda*), preferring to mumble to the air around him. Since nobody talked about this, I accepted it without question. Mostly Zayda was gone or sleeping anyway. For all the years I can remember, he worked nights at the Dodge Hotel, which seemed to be inhabited primarily by old men down on their luck.

Occasionally, when he worked the day shift, I begged to go with him. If he agreed, I would amuse myself in the lobby among the residents, who spent their afternoons sitting amid the palm trees and brass spittoons. One of the men knew a funny song he sang to me as he flicked his cigarette ashes into a spittoon: "Tor-ay ador-ay, don't spit on the floor-ay, use the cuspidor-ay, that's what it's for-ay."

On these days, Zayda remained lost in his thoughts behind the front desk. At home it was the same, except that he was lost in his thoughts sitting in his brown horsehair chair in the living room, staring out the window or reading a book, perpetually smoking one of his Wings cigarettes (or a cigarette he rolled himself), which he held gingerly between slender, yellow-stained fingers. A remote and silent presence in wire-rimmed glasses that magnified his soft brown eyes, he was inaccessible, a captive within his own invisible walls.

The fact that the Lake Street house was in an integrated neighborhood was of no interest to me. Most of our neighbors were black, not that anyone in my family would have called them "black" then. In those days, long before the Black Consciousness Movement, they would have said "Negro" or "colored"—or they might have used the Yiddish word "*shvartza*." I heard that word so often growing up that I came to understand it meant someone who was black; I didn't understand the word's derogatory connotations until much later.

I don't think my family use the term pejoratively. They just happened to speak Yiddish most of the time, and shvartza is a Jewish word. I don't remember any name-calling or racial incidents in our neighborhood. On the other hand, we rarely interacted with any of our neighbors, black or white. Bobo, admiring Mrs. Frederick's beautiful flowers on the other side of the picket fence, might occasionally aim a few halting words in her direction. Ray, on the other hand, had only to appear on our front porch to be invited two yards down to drink lemonade with Mr. Thomas, the policeman, who told him interesting stories about his job on the police force. I was never invited to join them, although I hung out noisily on our porch and sometimes practiced cartwheels in the front lawn, where I easily could be seen.

Who could have guessed that I would be the one to create an "incident" with possible racial overtones? In the fall of that year, I began my academic life. My first week in kindergarten was undistinguished, but by the second week, I realized I was going to be stuck with my irritating tablemate for the whole semester unless I could get rid of him.

I had no idea that pulling the chair out from under him as he tried to sit down, dumping him unceremoniously on the floor, and splitting the chair seat in the process was going to be such a big deal. As I explained to my mother, who was summoned to school immediately, he was a squirming, color-blind table-shaker who constantly poked crayons under my nose, asking, "Hey, what color is this one?"

My mother was not sympathetic. As we walked home together, she refused to listen to how he kept disturbing me and how I couldn't hear the teacher and how he wasn't worthy of her concern anyway. She grabbed me by the arm and yanked me along the sidewalk, landing an occasional well-placed jab here and there, which was actually a relief because when she was really mad, she pinched.

This squirming, color-blind table-shaker happened to be "colored," she pointed out, and my actions could have very serious consequences if anyone thought I pulled out his chair because he was colored and I was white. This is the only reference to racial issues I can remember. No serious consequences did occur. My color-blind tablemate was given a safer haven the next day, and the O'Brien children across the street, to whom I had provided the illustrated sexual romp by Popeye and Olive Oyl, were white Irish Catholics, and they never ratted on me.

Every house on Lake Street had a postage-stamp front yard and a porch that extended across the front of the house. The houses were deep, but only one or two rooms wide, resembling the "shotgun houses" of New Orleans, with which I would later become familiar.

My favorite time was in the evenings after dinner, when my uncles and I sat on the front porch together. They told me stories sometimes, but mostly they liked to teach me things—like how to find the Milky Way in the sky, or how to locate the North Star at the end of the Little Dipper. After they taught me to recognize the manufacturers of the cars that passed us by the shape of their radiator caps, it became our nightly game. I was expected to name the specific company of each car as soon as it appeared. I still remember that the ship with the sails was a Plymouth, the car with the naked lady and the streaming hair was a Packard, and the Indian head was a Pontiac.

During the day, when my uncles were gone, I pursued all my creative projects on the rug in the living room. The living room and dining room were one long room separated by an arch and wooden pillars. On the living room side of the arch were wooden bookcases with glass doors. In front of the doors were matching woven baskets on pedestals. The baskets were filled with yellow, orange, and green balls of crinkled cellophane. Although they looked like flowers when you squinted, I knew these "bouquets" were really fruit wrappers from the grocery store because they still smelled vaguely like citrus. These two bright accents provided the only color in the relentlessly brown room, reminding me of the rouge spots on our neighbor Mrs. Frederick's brown face.

The couch and two matching chairs in the living room were unadorned except for the doilies Bobo crocheted and strategically placed where dirty fingers or greasy heads might stray. The only concessions to adornment were Zayda's floor lamp, placed near the chair where he read, and my rug.

One of my ongoing projects was designing dresses for my paper dolls to wear to my tea parties in the attic. I designed their dresses by holding the dolls up to the window and tracing along their bodies on tissue paper. I colored in collars, sleeves, buttons, and belts, and then I cut them out. Cutting around the curves was tricky, and sometimes I became so absorbed, I forgot to add tabs at the shoulders and waist, which meant I couldn't attach the clothes to the dolls. When this happened, I tried fastening them with hairpins, but this never worked for long.

My best projects came the day the mailman brought us mail-order catalogs. These catalogs could keep me busy for days. "Amaze Your Friends! Be the Life of the Party!" the bold ads for magic books promised.

"Throw Your Voice! Astonish Your Friends! They Will Think the Lamp Is Talking!" another headline proclaimed. In the accompanying illustration, cartoon people indicated astonishment by standing with open mouths near a lamp surrounded by zigzag lines.

There were also gadgets to make you popular. One was a small, round object to conceal in your palm that buzzed when you shook hands with someone. (I didn't see how that could make you popular.) Another gadget looked like rubber tubes twisted together with handles. The ad for it said it would transform you from a "99-pound weakling" to someone no one would ever throw sand at again. I showed this to my skinny Uncle Ray, but he wasn't interested. As he pointed out, no one was going to throw sand at him because we didn't live anywhere near a beach.

I wasn't interested in being popular (this was destined to happen a few years later), so I quickly moved on to the pictures of watches and rings on the back pages of the catalogs. These were the things that interested me. With the arrival of every catalog, I sat for hours, painstakingly cutting out these pictures. If I did a perfect job, I imagined these objects would magically become real on my wrists and fingers. I never gave up hope. With each catalog, I would try again. (I attribute this irrational determination to my father, "Old Pressed-Lips," who never gave up on anything either. This probably also explains why I'm still buying anti-aging products from Walgreen's at the age of seventy-nine.)

On the other side of the pillars was the dining room. The only thing in this room was a long, oval table with a number of unmatched chairs around it. Aside from providing us with a place to eat, the table had other important functions: if you were in disfavor and could run around the table fast enough, you might avoid the "pinchers." Pinching was the punishment of choice on this side of the family. I learned this run-around-the-table trick from Ray, who was still getting into trouble regularly. Three times around the table usually worked, he said, and if you could make them laugh, you might get exonerated without needing to exhaust yourself.

The table also served as a learning center where, several times a week, a rabbi with a beard came to prepare Uncle Ray for his bar mitzvah. First, the two of them wrapped long, white scarves with fringe at the end around their necks. Then they opened small, plush bags and took out long, narrow leather straps with little black boxes on them. Wrapping these straps around their arms and foreheads, they rocked back and forth, singing words that didn't mean anything. I was an avid observer of this ritual, mimicking them every week until I could do it almost as well as Ray. He had his bar mitzvah at thirteen, but if given the opportunity and a stool, I could have performed credibly at five.

From the dining room, one archway led to the bedrooms, the other to the big sunny kitchen, Bobo's domain. When she was working in the kitchen, I was never far away. When she baked, I licked the pans; when she got out her wooden rolling pin, I helped her roll dough into long, stringy noodles; when she sewed, I helped her thread the bobbins, watching as her slippered feet pumped the treadle up and down while her gnarled fingers directed the cloth.

During one of these sessions, she measured me with her yardstick and made me a beautiful navy-blue dress with tiny, red flowers. In my opinion, she was a much better magician than Rumpelstiltskin. She could turn shapeless material into a dress with a lacy collar and a matching sash, while he could only spin straw into gold.

On washdays, we were very busy. Bobo washed clothes in a large alcove just off the kitchen. I helped her fill the big tub with soapy bubbles. Then, getting out her corrugated metal washboard, she pressed her slim body against it and rubbed the clothes across its ridges until rivulets of soapy water, like beaten egg whites, spilled down the gray metal. After she squeezed out the water with a wringer attached to a smaller tub, we carried the clothes to the clothesline in the backyard. My job was to hand her the clothespins, one at a time, when she held out her hand.

The year my mother and I lived in Omaha, we shared the front bedroom, sleeping together in the big bed pushed up against the longest wall. Along the opposite wall, next to the door, was a carved wood vanity with drawers and a large round mirror. When Mother was going out, she sat on the matching bench to put on her makeup. Together we stared into the mirror, studying her image. As I watched, she transformed herself into a glamorous movie star. With her eyes sparkling and a small beauty mark carefully penciled on near the corner of her curvy mouth, she seemed as beautiful as Ruby Keeler or Jean Harlow or any of the other Hollywood stars in my Uncle Max's glossy picture collection.

During the day, Mother worked in the office of Mr. Resnick's Coal Company. I was obsessed with the idea of going to work with her. Every night, she promised to take me with her if I happened to be awake when she left. I tried falling asleep clutching her arm and twisting my leg around hers, but she was always gone when I woke up in the morning.

I still wish I could have gone with her. I would have enjoyed reliving the memory of her typing and filing and sitting at her own desk. It was her only real job, as far as

I know, a tentative move toward independence. I have thought how different her life might have turned out if she had inherited her mother's ambition instead of her father's passivity. Would she then have been so desperate to escape the ongoing drama between her parents that she would elope at the age of sixteen?

It was Bobo who kept my world afloat that year. I had immunity from any storm that might be gathering strength in the puckers of her perpetually furrowed brow. Her love for me was unconditional—a favored status I was to enjoy throughout her life.

We were partners in the day-to-day routine, but when it came to the Sabbath, our workload doubled. Preparing for the Sabbath took two days. It began with Bobo scrubbing the kitchen floor on her hands and knees and then spreading newspapers over the floor to keep it clean. Not only did the Sabbath require a spotless kitchen, it also demanded a special dinner. For that, we made our weekly pilgrimage to 24th Street.

Our trips always began with the same ritual: Bobo would gather together her round box of Coty powder, her comb, and her brush, placing them all neatly on the oilcloth that covered the kitchen table. Next, she would fetch her pewter mirror, which tilted on its pewter stand. The hole in the stand was meant to hold a shaving mug, she said. Tilting the mirror to examine her face, she released her lava-black hair from its restraining bun at the back of her neck and brushed until it crackled with static electricity; then, deftly, she twisted it back into a bun. (Unlike the rest of us, who all turned gray early, her hair remained black until she died, sometime late in her seventies).

After Bobo powdered her face—she used no other makeup—she replaced her cotton housedress with a "going-out" dress, usually black and belted, and checked her reflection in the full-length mirror behind her closet door. Not quite five feet tall, straight and slim (she was probably a size zero), she sought perfection. If she were going anywhere besides shopping on 24th Street—a very rare occasion—she would consult the *maven*, my mother, her thoroughly modern daughter who knew about such things. But just for shopping, she was satisfied with her own careful inspection. At the front door, she stepped out of her old house slippers and into a pair of sturdy black oxfords with two-inch heels. Then we walked to the street corner, climbed the steep steps of the streetcar, and headed for 24th Street.

One of the best things about the day was riding in the clanging streetcar with its reversible cane benches and the intriguing signs posted above the windows: "Zig-Zag Rolling Paper—Quality You Can Trust," "Don't Spit on the Floor, It's Against the Law," and, of course, the ubiquitous Doublemint twins, who could "Double Your Pleasure, Double Your Fun," if you just chewed their gum.

As the streetcar rocked along the tracks, making its way up and down the Omaha hills, we watched the world go by. Occasionally a streetcar going in the opposite direction flashed a quick reflection of blurry faces sitting in a car like ours, and then the parade of small houses and tidy yards resumed. When houses gave way to stores and gas stations with green or red pumps topped with winged horses or regal crowns, it was time for me to stand up and pull the overhead rope. We had arrived.

On the sidewalks outside the shops were barrels of pickles, fragrant with dill and garlic, and baskets of colorful fruits and vegetables, previews of what could be purchased inside. The bakery windows were especially enticing: tantalizing displays of *schnecken* (spiral-shaped pastries with nuts and cinnamon, sometimes called sticky buns), *challah* (twisted leavened bread baked especially for the Sabbath), and *hamantaschen,* (three-cornered pastries filled with prunes, preserves, or poppy seeds, and associated with Purim). Accompanying this display was the seductive smell of freshly baked bread. No less compelling were the windows of the meat market, filled with thinly sliced corned beef and elegant briskets.

Shoppers carrying sacks stuffed with loaves of bread and butcher paper packages greeted each other in Yiddish. Cheerful smiles were exchanged. Everyone seemed to know everyone else on 24th Street, and they all seemed to be shopping for their Sabbath dinner.

Despite the hustle and bustle in the street, formalities were observed inside the stores. I was introduced in every shop as Bobo's *anical* (grandchild), an announcement that was always received with approving nods and smiles in my direction. That was the end of the foreplay, now Bobo was all business. She studied the proffered merchandise, sometimes accepting it, other times pointing to something else in the showcase. I occupied myself by blowing on the slanted glass cases and writing my name in the fog with my wet finger, careful to erase everything with my sleeve when we were ready to leave. If these exchanges took too long, and I grew restless and impatient, Bobo might placate me with a sour pickle or, even better, a caramel apple.

I recalled these trips to 24th Street many years later, when I visited Bobo in Venice Beach, California, where she had moved after the dedication of Zayda's gravestone, about a year after his death. Despite their troubles while he was alive, she genuinely mourned Zayda's passing and cried bitterly at his funeral. It was not like Bobo to show her feelings so publicly; I realized then how deeply she had been invested in their relationship, whatever it had been.

We were all surprised when Bobo announced that she was going to sell her house and move to California. She had lived in Omaha ever since her arrival from Poland. No one could remember her traveling anywhere else. But now, she said, the Omaha winters were too much for her. She couldn't work in the yard anymore, and nobody in Omaha needed her: my mother was living in New Orleans, Ray was married and busy with his law practice, and Max had already moved to California, settling not too far from Bobo's cousin, a *landsman* (a fellow Jew from the same shtetl in Europe). He had bought some real estate there, she said. Maybe she would buy something too.

Over the years in Omaha, Bobo had continued to flex her entrepreneurial muscle. With every house she bought, lived in, and then sold, she made a small profit, depositing her gains in whatever financial institution offered her the highest interest rate. If small repairs or a little paint would elevate her profit, she could always depend on Max, who was handy with tools.

She continued this practice after she moved to California. With Max's help and her cousin's knowledge of California real estate, she invested her *knipple* (secret savings), in a duplex in Hollywood and settled herself in Venice Beach, close to her cousin's synagogue and not far from Max. Assisted by inflation and a modest lifestyle, her assets grew steadily. She lived comfortably in Venice Beach for the rest of her life—even managing to leave a small estate to each of her three children (not bad for a late-blooming "greenhorn," as she called herself).

The day I visited her there—sometime in the late sixties—turned out to be the last time I ever saw her. We had not been together since she moved to California many years before. During this interval, I had married, moved to Iowa, and had three children.

I remember that day in Venice Beach vividly. She lived in a sunny stucco apartment building with a red tile roof. I felt uneasy as I rang her doorbell. How many years had it been since we saw each other? Would we be able to talk to each other? We kissed and hugged awkwardly. As she ushered me into her cheerful living room, I was happy to see how little she had changed (same black hair in a bun, same size-zero body).

Glancing around her living room, I recognized the oval picture of her grandmother. It was still hanging in its place of honor over the small chest she had brought from Europe. I suspected I would find the pewter mirror if I poked around in her drawers, probably wrapped in tissue paper somewhere.

If I had been filming our day together, I wouldn't have

needed a sound track. I had forgotten most of my Yiddish, and her English hadn't gotten any better. Without my mother or my uncles to translate for us, we were reduced to gestures and a sprinkling of mutually understood words. Once in a while, we managed to connect, sparking smiles and knowing nods.

She quickly assumed the familiar role of hostess, preparing lunch for me as she had done so many times when I was a child. Out of the refrigerator came a carton of cottage cheese and a tomato. She buttered a piece of challah and cut up an apple. We munched silently, sitting at a small table near the counter that divided the kitchen from the living room. After this simple meal, she turned on the television set and motioned to me to sit on the couch. She didn't want me to help her gather the plates or bring them into the small kitchen. The kitchen was still her domain.

As I watched television, she washed and stacked the dishes in the rack near the sink. Her dishwasher remained, as usual, unused. Bobo always had a way of living on top of things. She had never used the dishwashers in any of her houses; it was too much trouble, she always said, but I think she was "saving" them—the way she saved her furniture and lampshades under plastic coverings.

After lunch, she wanted to take a walk. She walked slowly, but she was as straight and as trim as ever. Properly dressed and shod, we walked along on the sidewalk close to the beach and the neighborhood shops. She introduced me to the grocer and the baker in Yiddish and held brief conversations with each of them. I heard the word *anical*; it was one word I still understood. She bought some oranges, which I insisted on carrying as we slowly made our way back to her apartment.

Walking with her that day in Venice Beach, I realized she had found another 24th Street in California. Venice Beach in the sixties was a diverse hodgepodge of humanity, a seamless yet disparate patchwork quilt of the young and the old, the dressed and the practically undressed, commingling with ease. On the sidewalks, robust old people competed for space with ubiquitous roller skaters. Near the water, people exercised or simply sat in the sun. Musicians—alone and in groups—played liquid refrains that floated in the warm air. The music, accompanied by the babbling sounds of Yiddish, Russian, and English, was a fugue of discordant yet oddly harmonious elements.

Back in Bobo's apartment, we took the same places as before, but this time we watched the news on television together. As we listened, a local bank advertised its new interest rate. Bobo managed to make me understand that it was a better rate than she was getting. I was pleased to see she was still keeping up with the world of interest rates.

Several years after my visit with Bobo, I read an outstanding book called *Number Our Days,* in which Barbara Myerhoff, a noted anthropologist, described her work with the Jews of Venice Beach. She was interested in finding successful aging strategies within an ethnic group, and she had chosen a cluster of feisty eighty- to ninety-year-olds as her study group.

From her book, I learned that Venice Beach was once a thriving Jewish community of 10,000 mostly Ashkenazic Jews from Eastern Europe, like Bobo. By the time Bobo moved there, the Jewish population had dwindled to a few hundred. Myerhoff 's conclusion about her study group was comforting. She believed her spunky old Jews were continuously revitalized by their shared ethnicity and *mamaloshen* (mother tongue).

When I reflect on the risks Bobo took throughout her life, I am amazed by her courage and her confidence in herself. Her entrepreneurial spirit never failed her. It even led her to a community where she could spend her final days with a feisty bunch of old Jews in shared ethnicity. I still regret that I didn't have mamaloshen to offer her that last day we were together. I have never forgotten the heavy silence that enshrouded us. I wanted so much to string some Yiddish words together to tell her how much she had meant to me. I am left with the dim hope that somewhere, in a place beyond words, she knew.

Not long after Bobo died, I divorced and moved to California myself. It was my own personal immigration. I also left everything familiar and everyone I loved in the hopes of finding a better life—one I hoped would lead to gainful employment—gainful enough for me to earn a living for the first time in my forty-something life. To accomplish this, I enrolled in a two-and-a-half-year photography school in Santa Barbara that offered a bachelor's degree in a variety of specialties.

My solution to an ending has been to go back to school. I think it's my way of turning an ending into a beginning. Somewhere between my divorce and my enrollment in Brooks Institute, Mother chose to reveal the secrets she had kept to herself for years: We were living in Omaha that year, she said, because my father had abandoned us. I was stunned. Why?

Because, she answered with a certain amount of the venom she still felt, he had some frivolous dream of becoming a professional singer in Chicago. Imagine, a married man with a child! Totally irresponsible! She had filed for divorce over the objections of her family, especially Bobo, who had always liked my father, perhaps because he was ambitious, unlike her husband.

With Mother's revelation, I suddenly understood it all: why my father hadn't been there that year; why Mother had gone to work at Resnick's Coal Company; why those gentleman callers had come to visit. The story left me sad for both for them. It was easy to sympathize with my mother, but my father had an extraordinary baritone voice. Shouldn't he have had the chance to see where his dream might take him?

Maslow's theory of self-actualization may have fallen into disfavor, but I couldn't help wishing my father could have climbed a little higher on Maslow's "hierarchy of needs" ladder. I never discussed this bit of marital history with my father. We were all too far along in our lives by the time I found out about it. I know he found a job in Chicago singing in a bar that proclaimed itself to be "The Longest Bar in the World." He kept a book of matches from there in his top drawer for many years.

I'm not sure how long he was gone. His *narishkeit* (foolishness) ended when his mother boarded a bus to Chicago and brought him back. Despite her mild manner, my other grandmother—whose name sounded like Hodel, but may have been spelled Odell—could gather supernatural strength when one of her children threatened to wander off the straight and narrow. Usually the wanderer was her son George, my father, a maverick way back to his Russian days. (It took her death to "tame" him, but that's another chapter.)

I'm not sure why my mother picked this particular time to tell me the story of my father's desertion, but I think it was because she disapproved of my divorce. Perhaps she felt that I was demonstrating the same unreasonable willfulness as my father.

I may not remember if I missed my father that year, but I do remember the drama of his sudden reappearance: I had the mumps. I was lying on the scratchy couch in the living room, which was covered by a sheet to protect it from the thick, black salve Bobo had smeared all over my swollen cheeks. A red bandanna, tied at the top of my head, covered the gooey mess. Mother was working. Bobo and I were alone in the house when the doorbell rang.

After a brief conversation with Bobo at the door, my father carried me out of the house and into his old truck. He said we were going to Sioux City. His truck rattled over the unpaved road and smelled vaguely of fish. Then he carried me, still wrapped in Bobo's sheet, up the wooden steps to my grandparents' apartment above their fish market.

I don't remember anything after that. I'm sure there were persuasive arguments by both sides of the family in favor of their getting back together. They were probably ready to reconcile anyway. The divorce was never final.

One secret would have been *dayenu* (according to our Passover Haggadah, it means "it would have been sufficient"), but Mother knew another secret. Bobo had been married to someone else before she married Zayda.

That marriage had been a "love match," my mother said, not arranged by a matchmaker. This was so astonishing, I had a hard time listening to the rest of the story. They had been married only a short time when her first husband died, my mother continued. She guessed it was probably during the cholera epidemic that swept through Europe. Nobody else knew about this, she added, not even my uncles.

Bobo's marriage to Zayda had not only been "arranged," they had never even seen each other before they were married. It had been considered a good match—a joint venture between a worldly family (Bobo's) with a scholar (Zayda). Perhaps this admixture was good for the long-term economic and religious survival of Judaism, but for Jacob and Sarah it was a disaster, one they chose to live with, to the discomfort of everybody concerned.

This secret life of Bobo's made me wonder if I had ever really known her. Why had she kept this from everyone but my mother, not even telling her two sons? What other secrets did my mother know that she wasn't telling?

Mother told Ray and Max after she told me. Ray said it made him question whether Max and my mother were the other man's children. He decided that Mother, at least, had so many of Zayda's personality traits, he must be her father. I didn't point out that the traits he was identifying—passivity at the top of the list—could be ascribed to "nurture" as well as "nature."

Although my mother adored Zayda, she never told me enough about him to make him more than a shadowy figure in the family story. I knew he had been a respected teacher and a biblical scholar who had enjoyed respect and entitlements in the shtetl, but these honors did not translate into the ability to make a living in America.

Landing in Galveston as Jacob Samueltitsky, he left Galveston as Jacob Simon, transformed by a stroke of a lazy or uncomprehending immigration agent's hand. We figured later that this might have been the result of a garbled reference to the town of Siemianowice Slaskie, Poland, from which we think he emigrated.

Unlike most immigrants to America, Zayda had no relatives in this country and no sponsor. A chance friendship with a fellow immigrant led him from Galveston to Omaha, where he undertook a series of mostly low-paying and uninteresting jobs. We know he went into business with a partner once, making hamburgers and sandwiches somewhere near a factory, and that he worked briefly for the WPA, the government agency that created jobs during the Great Depression. Ray once told me he could remember Zayda leaving the house in darkness, dressed in overalls, and returning in darkness, exhausted and covered with grime.

My scholarly grandfather could never have been a good match for Bobo's tireless, driving nature. Passive and remote, he withstood the onslaught of her invectives over the years with stony silence, retreating into the safety of his thoughts or his books. Most of the books I found in their houses had been his. During the summers we spent with them, I read them all. They were mostly adventure stories about heroic men, westerns by Zane Grey and classics like *Beau Geste* and *The Four Feathers*. Perhaps Zayda chose to dream himself into a more audacious life, like Thurber's Walter Mitty.

I believe my grandparents loved each other, although

I personally never saw evidence of it. I asked Ray once if he ever saw them kissing or hugging each other. He said that when he was six or seven, he had wandered into the kitchen and caught Zayda pinching Bobo on her behind as she bent to open the oven door. I marvel at this image; it made me regret I didn't try harder to penetrate Zayda's walls. We could have discussed his books, I might have asked him about his life in Poland.

I would have had that chance on one of the occasions when Zayda came to visit us, always by himself. I don't remember my mother and Zayda having long conversations, but I know she always drove him to the bus station or the train station, where he would remain for hours, just watching the comings and goings, until it was time for Mother to pick him up. Was he imagining the lives of the passengers he watched? Had he ever been tempted to leave us and go off somewhere alone?

Perhaps my mother never penetrated Zayda's walls either, but I know she thought about her father every day, at least once, after he died. Before we realized the dangers associated with cigarettes, she told me she smoked a cigarette for him every morning when she drank her coffee.

As it turned out, it was Bobo I thought of most often during the years I lived in California. In the darkroom, where I spent countless hours breathing the acrid air and observing varicosities explode along my aching legs, I thought of her strength, her tenacity, her daring. She became my role model during those years when I struggled to support myself, intent on penetrating the mysteries of the world of money and finance.

I gathered courage from her example: Hadn't she come alone to this country, with just my mother and Max? Without formal education, hadn't she been able to learn and implement the principles of leverage and interest rates, even managing to leave a knipple behind for her three children? I knew her genetic legacy was implanted somewhere inside of me because my toes were just like hers. I was standing on the shoulders—with the toes—of a giant who was not quite five feet tall. So how could I fail?

The Fish Market

"Jesus was a Jew, yes, but only on his mother's side."
—Archie Bunker

Fortunately for me, my father's family provided a sharp contrast to the complicated, brooding relationships on my mother's side. The Schulmans were like Flip Wilson's character, Geraldine: WYSIWYG (What You See Is What You Get). They were outgoing, good-natured, and full of affection for each other. The contrast between the two families was sharp: the difference between a song written in a major key and one written in a minor key; a story by Dave Barry compared with one by Edgar Allen Poe. Importantly, the Schulmans gave me a sense of belonging to what I perceived to be a normal family. This was before the age of family sitcoms, so my experience with normal families was limited, but I think I imagined "normal" to be something like a Jewish Cleaver family.

The Schulman family's get-togethers took place in the apartment above my grandparents' fish market in Sioux City, Iowa. Every Jewish holiday was an occasion for a family reunion, to be observed and celebrated by all of my father's siblings and their offspring. When my aunts, uncles, and cousins descended from all over the country to occupy the maze of small rooms where my grandparents lived, it made for some startling sleeping arrangements—particularly after one fertile period when our offspring total seemed to increase exponentially. And with one bathroom, forget privacy. There was always someone waiting, and the door didn't lock.

Despite these inconveniences, our family reunions were among the happiest days of my childhood. With the Simons, my mother's family, it was brooding silence—Heathcliff on the moors. With the Schulmans it was: "Tumult! Projects! Singing!" Plus there were all those cousins, three glamorous aunts, a talented uncle, and my grandparents—the loving alpha dogs—who made all this possible.

The assets my grandfather brought with him to Sioux City were his affability and sharp wit. These characteristics may not be moneymaking skills, but they are the qualities that distinguished him and enriched our lives. I consider them his greatest legacy.

My grandmother, on the other hand, was reserved and hardworking, a shepherdess tending her flock. On the few occasions when a lamb managed to drift off temporarily—two elopements come to mind—she successfully lassoed and roped them back in line. To her family, she was imbued with the same indescribable quality possessed by the Dog Whisperer, with a dash of the commanding presence of Horace Rumpole's wife, Hilda, who also "must be obeyed."

These grandparents were very religious. Everybody called my grandfather "Reb Mayer," even his children, and proper observance of all Jewish rituals was nonnegotiable and never questioned. Reb Mayer was not only a scholar in the old country, he was one of a long line of Jewish scholars, which included his mystical grandfather—a holy man so powerful, he could exorcise a *dybbuk*.

Big in Jewish folklore and Jewish literature, a dybbuk is a homeless soul caught between two worlds who must find and inhabit the body of a living person until it works out its karma and is finally released to transmigrate on—kind of a Jewish version of reincarnation. My cousins and I knew that only rabbis with very special abilities could extricate such a buttinsky. We grew up awed by the stories told about our great-great-great-great-grandfather's power. He was known far and wide, we were told, as "the linen rabbi," because of his elegant robe. Although I heard Zayda had brought a precious remnant of this cloth to America, I never actually saw it. This did not stop me from believing in the linen rabbi and his powers.

I often imagined what it might look like when my great-great-great-great-grandfather forcibly ejected a dybbuk. Years later, my mother took me to see a movie called *The Dybbuk,* and I didn't have to imagine it anymore. Although the movie was in Yiddish, which I barely understood, I could tell when the dybbuk was exorcised from the girl's body because she stopped talking in a guttural male voice and everyone in the movie clapped and grew ecstatic.

The dybbuk may have floated over the victim before disappearing in a puff of smoke. Since the movie was distributed in 1938 and I was seven, some of the details have escaped me. Still, that movie haunted me for a long time—particularly at bedtime, when I imagined dybbuks buzzing around my bed like mosquitoes, looking for a way to enter my body and inhabit my soul.

Coming from such a distinguished family, my grandfather was deemed appropriate—by the authorities that deem these things—to marry into my grandmother's relatively prosperous Hochman family. According to my father, they were shopkeepers who owned several businesses along the main street in Petrikov.

It was an excellent match. My grandmother was the love of Zayda's life. In addition to her lassoing and herding abilities, she was a strong, selfless woman, stoutly built, who seemed to toil endlessly on behalf her family, all of whom adored her and spoke of her in reverent tones. (If Jews could be saints, I'm absolutely sure her family would have nominated her for canonization.)

My grandfather's first job in Sioux City was working for the Jewish butcher. According to Zayda—who told great stories and loved to tell this one—he reported to work on his first day, crestfallen to learn he was expected to deliver meat to the butcher's customers.

"But I can't read English," he protested. "How will I find your customers?"

"Don't worry," the butcher reassured him, as he filled his cart with packages. "The horse knows the way. He'll take you to all the right places. My customers will recognize the cart and take the packages with their names on it."

Zayda paused, "The butcher should have paid the horse. He was smarter than I was!"

Over the years, my grandparents managed to save enough money to open a fish market on the west side of Sioux City. It was an ideal location for all of us: across the street from the movie theater and just a block or two from their orthodox synagogue, an easy walk to Sabbath services.

To their grandchildren, the apartment above the store was more than a place to hold our family reunions. It was a virtual theme park of activities that included dance marathons to music supplied by the wind-up Victrola in the living room, endless crannies in which to play hide-and-go-seek, treasure hunts among the storage boxes piled up on the back porch behind the kitchen, and any other ideas we could dream up.

When the family assembled for the holidays, they arrived from New York, Detroit, Chicago, and the nearby town of Walnut, Iowa, where my favorite cousin Bob, my co-conspirator and fellow explorer, lived. Although he lived closer than anyone else, I remember spending a lot of time on the sidewalk in front of the fish market, in growing darkness, waiting for my Aunt Helen's car to appear.

Waiting was boring, but I challenged myself to keep busy. I stared through the big front window into the store, watching my grandfather as he cleaned fish or waited on a customer. Then I changed focus and stared at my reflection; although I was now nine or ten, I was still a skinny kid with knobby knees and braids. Not much to see there.

Next I ran my finger over the letters "TODAY'S SPECIAL," written with a chalk-like marker on the outside of the window; it felt cool and slick. My attention now switched to the sticky substance I had just deposited on my finger, which I tried to wipe off on the front of my shirt. Raising my head, I stared at the green neon tubes that spelled “FISH MARKET” just inside the window. I noted that some of the green was missing, leaving a large gap between the words. Where did it go?

It was dark enough now for the big sign to be turned on. The big sign, attached by heavy brackets to the brick wall above my head, was shaped like a giant fish outlined in red neon. When it blinked on and off, the fish appeared and disappeared in the darkness.

As I waited, I thought of things Bob and I could do for the next few days. I imagined elaborate webs of intrigue. We might be detectives in search of a desperate criminal lurking somewhere in the empty lot behind the store where abandoned junk cars, torn upholstery, and rusted springs offered endless possibilities for hiding. Or we might be escaped prisoners, on the other side of the law, eluding the police among the large containers piled high in the back room behind the store.

The back room also had a desk with office machines, offering alternative possibilities. Using the check machine, we might imprint a pink check for a million dollars by pressing the top and bottom of the check machine together to produce a thin and embossed pink waffle. Or we might try typing a fan letter to Clark Gable or Carole Lombard on the old Underwood typewriter—if we could keep the keys from sticking together in the pit in the middle.

Along the back of the room, near the giant scale, was the freight elevator that could be lowered to the basement by pulleys. We weren’t allowed go down there alone; we had to wait for our grandfather to make the jerky subterranean voyage to the damp world below. When we got down there, we would usually inch our way carefully on the wet, slippery floor and head for the huge tank of wriggling fish. Pressing our knees against the metal, we watched the fish until our knees grew so cold they ached.

Nearby were the ominous locked rooms known as "the cooler" and "the freezer." Only occasionally did we accompany our grandfather into these icy chambers, where—in just an instant—our arms and legs erupted with goose bumps and our breath turned to vapor. Hanging by giant hooks above our heads were huge fish so crusted with ice they had turned into shapeless monsters, which we had to stoop and turn sideways to avoid.

I ran out of ideas about the time Zayda turned on the big fish sign. If Aunt Helen and Bob still weren't there, and if there were no customers, I would go inside and persuade Zayda to let me put on my roller skates and glide across the worn linoleum floor while he cleaned fish behind the counters.

Skating around the white enamel showcases, I stopped occasionally to observe the neat rows of gray scaly fish separated by hedges of ice. Each fish lay on an icy bed, its sightless eye fixed on the fish ahead in a cold, gray parade. Coming closer, I examined the evil whiskers of the catfish, admired the paddle-shaped bluegills, and stared into the gaping mouths of the bass.

When I grew tired of this motionless drama, I took off the skates and walked behind the counters on the curly sawdust, which muffled my footsteps and clung to the rims of my shoes. I stood close to Zayda's wooden bucket, staring as he cleaned the fish, transfixed by the falling scales that mutated into a shower of dull sequins. With one deft stroke of his knife, Zayda split the fish open, revealing its pink, glistening interior. He handed me the luminous gills. Still plump with air, they made a very satisfactory pop when I stomped on them with my sawdust-covered shoes.

If a customer happened to come in, I would retreat to the fish tank by the front door. It was a miniature version of the big one in the basement. As I watched the torpid fish circling the tank, I thought of my younger cousins, several of whom had fallen into the tank. I leaned over the tank slightly, imagining how it would feel to lose my balance and fall into the cold water, surrounded by slimy fish. I shuddered. Ray said when you shudder, it means someone was walking over your grave. I didn't understand this since I wasn't dead, but if Ray said it, it must be true. I pictured my grave. Did they ever make a mistake and bury someone who wasn't quite dead?

After his customer left, Zayda and I sat together on the wooden chairs arranged in front of the map of the United States that his younger son, our Uncle Harry, had painted on the wall. The map looked just like the ones in my geography book. The pale green land mass began up near the ceiling, where Uncle Harry had outlined the Canadian border, and continued down the wall to Florida, just inches above the floor. Only the bright blue fingers of the Great Lakes interrupted the green mass, while the skinny blue crack of the Mississippi River continued to trickle down the wall, to empty into the crescent-shaped Gulf of Mexico.

While we waited for Aunt Helen and Bob, Zayda read his prayer book, his lips silently moving, his *yarmulke* (skull cap) slipping to one side of his head. Slowly, his eyelids closed, and his head drooped. His breath erupted into loud snores, but I could never be sure he was really sleeping. Sometimes he just pretended, and if I wandered close to his chair, he might grab and capture me and hold me prisoner between his knees or wrap me in his strong arms and carry me around the store while I thrashed and kicked like a fish in a net.

When Aunt Helen's car finally appeared in front of the store, Zayda locked up and we climbed the steep wooden stairs, the welcoming smells of soup and roasting chicken growing stronger as we climbed.

We usually found the grownups congregated around the round oak table in the dining room. The dining room was the hub of the apartment. No one ever sat in the living room, although it was light and cheerful and had two long windows that overlooked the street. The only reason to be in the living room was to go to sleep—on the long couch that opened into the bed where we children slept horizontally so more of us could fit—or to play the Victrola.

The Victrola was a big draw for my cousins and me. An eclectic collection of waxy brown records was stored in its lower cabinet. The records were mostly Jewish music. One odd record had no music at all; it was just the voice of a man telling jokes. After each joke, a woman laughed. Her laugh got weaker and weaker until, at the end, she gasps and there is silence. My mother said it was about a man who kills his wife with laughter. Could that really happen, I wondered? Could you die if you laughed too hard?

My cousins and I just played the records we could dance to. The best ones were "Three Little Words" and "Pennies from Heaven." Inside the hinged top of the Victrola was a picture of a spotted dog next to a giant horn. We took turns placing the record on the spindle and cranking the handle on the side of the Victrola until it wouldn't move any more.

As the needle scratched its way across the wavy grooves, the record rose and fell under the horizontal arm. At the beginning of the record, the high, screechy voices sounded as though they were filled with helium gas, but all too soon the music slowed to a dirge. Matching the music's tempo, we hopped, we loped, we lurched, and finally staggered to the floor, the needle continuing to scratch along the surface of the record until one of us finally got up and took the record off.

When the grownups had about as much of this as they could take, we had to find another way to occupy ourselves. I usually went into our grandparents' bedroom because I was allowed to play with the jewelry my grandmother kept in a big tin box on her dresser.

In the box were narrow gold rings with tiny, sparkling stones, a glittering brooch that separated into two clips, a peacock pin, silver and turquoise hair combs, ropes of pearls, and strings of shining black beads. There was also an American flag pin with diamonds for stars. Not one for subtlety, I usually put on everything—my chest and fingers heavy with jewels—strutting around the adults still sitting at the dining room table, waiting for them to notice and admire me.

Most of the time at these reunions, the aunts stayed home together, cooking or sewing or working on a project, but sometimes they wanted to get dressed and go shopping. At these times, they would buy tickets for the movie across the street, buy us popcorn, and deposit us in our seats. That gave them a whole afternoon of freedom, because theaters then showed two movies back-to-back, called double features. Although we were instructed to go outside and wait for them when we had seen both movies, we usually tried to watch the movies again, glued to our seats until a grownup finally showed up in the darkened theater to drag us home.

No matter what anybody did during the day, we were all expected to be together for dinner. Dinner was important, especially on Friday night. Since the table wasn't big enough for everyone, we ate in shifts. But whether we were in the first shift or the last one, it was mandatory that we all assemble for the prayers that preceded the meal. My grandmother would cover her head, light the candles, raise her cupped hands to her face, and softly whisper the familiar Hebrew words through her fingers. Then she would turn to my grandfather, who would contribute his vigorous additions, after which we all joined in for the concluding and boisterous amen.

Even when it wasn't the Sabbath, preparing for dinner could sometimes take the whole day, with all the aunts participating. Without resorting to hyperbole, I would describe these dinners as feasts. Delicious smells began to drift from the kitchen right after breakfast. There was almost always soup with something in it: *lokshen* (noodles, homemade), *borscht* (beets or spinach), *schav* (a chilled soup with sorrel), or *einlauf* (egg-drop dumplings).

Roasted chicken or brisket followed the soup, along with various *kugels* (noodles or potato puddings) and vegetables. Last, but certainly not least, were the deserts: mandelbrot, sponge cake, honey cake, and cookies of every description, all baked by the aunts and appearing on trays nightly.

After dinner, still sitting around the table, there was sure to be singing. The Schulmans took seriously the command "Make a joyful noise unto the Lord." I looked forward to these musical interludes because everyone loved to sing and everyone was a star. Zayda, who often assisted the cantor in his synagogue, might begin it. He sang boldly, with authority and enthusiasm, the way he lived. Then the resonant voices of my father, his sister Elsie, and his brother Harry would join in. When the three of them sang, everyone else listened, even Zayda.

Despite the merging of their voices, I could easily unravel the vocal strands: my father, a commanding baritone took—or was given—the lead, Aunt Elsie's trained soprano glided above him, as clear as broth, and Uncle Harry's warm, engaging tenor slid into a spot between them. Requests for solos, always forthcoming, might produce an hour of songs, in Yiddish and in English, interrupted by anecdotes and laughter and an occasional, "No, no, it goes like this."

My father's signature song was "My Yiddishe Mama." They were sure to request it. The way he sang it, it became an aria, a tragic story of deep sorrow and regret. After my grandmother died, he could never bring himself to sing it again.

He was deeply affected by her death. At that time, my parents belonged to Touro Synagogue, a reform synagogue not far from their apartment in New Orleans. Almost immediately, my father joined the small orthodox synagogue, Chevra Tillim, to say *Kaddish* (the prayer recited for a deceased relative) for her every day. After the required eleven months, he continued to go every morning.

He seemed to grow more observant with the passing years. What was it that drew him? Could it be an emotional umbilical cord that connected him to his past? He told me once he could remember—better than Zayda could—the way his grandfather in Russia had chanted certain prayers, and that was the way he chanted them too.

Perhaps he thought he was he was doing all this for my grandmother, but listening to him sing—his voice so eloquent and so professional—I believe it was the way he resolved, perhaps even rectified, his missed opportunity in Chicago.

But there was another star sitting around the table participating in these songfests: Elsie's husband, Ike Babbitt, was a bona fide performer. He could harmonize, improvise, and segue into clever parodies he had written without a moment's hesitation. He once appeared on "Major Bowe's Capitol Family Hour," a popular national radio show of the late 1930s, playing his one-man band—a feat that raised him to celebrity status, at least to the children of the family.

Once he brought his instruments to Sioux City and played "Hold That Tiger" for us, during which he blew on his horn to produce a tiger-like roar, while his hands beat the drums forcefully, and his feet pumped up and down on the cymbals. We were transfixed! Artistic talent ran in his family. His brother, Art, was a prominent animator and director for Walt Disney. (Tributes to Art Babbitt can still be found on YouTube. Googling him brings up page after page of accolades.)

After the songfest, on hot summer evenings, everyone would troop down the stairs to gather on the sidewalk in front of the fish market. Pulling out chairs and boxes from the store and fanning themselves with newspapers, the grownups sat and talked while we children, enveloped in the comforting flow of Yiddish, listened and grew sleepy.

As the grownups reminisced about their early lives, I watched the sky change from rosy pink to royal purple. Sometimes I imagined that I was with them in Petrikov. I could see Aunt Helen standing on a box to reach the cash register in the *krom* (store), and I could almost taste the spoonful of warm milk from the pot simmering on the brick oven, given to them by their loving grandmother, Bubbe Devonia. I could even feel the hard benches they endured in Hebrew school, but their stories about the arrogant soldiers who patrolled the streets and sometimes broke into their house to confiscate their treasures were beyond my imagination. Why didn't the police put them in jail? Worst of all were the stories about the loss of their sister, Slava (between Lillian and Elsie), who died of cholera before they left Russia for America.

If they got on the subject of the voyage to America, Zayda's dramatic journey, which took him from Russia across the frozen tundra of Siberia into China, was certain to come up. Almost penniless by the time he got to China, uncertain about what to do next, Zayda was saved from certain disaster by a series of miraculous events. There was the appearance of a passport forger who beckoned to him from a window and was willing to work for the pittance Zayda could pay him. And the woman he met in the street, who offered to guide him to the train that would take him to the boat leaving for America. Most miraculous of all, was the arrival of unexpected money by wire—just enough to complete his journey. This story always ended with a long, impenetrable silence followed by ruminations over unanswerable questions: Where had the money come from? Who could have known Zayda was hiding in that little wooden house with the chickens in the back yard? With such miracles, could there be a doubt about God's existence?

The aunts might chime in with their own dramatic escape story. Spotted by soldiers the first time they tried to leave Petrikov, they waited two years before trying it again. This time they left in a horse-drawn wagon totally covered by blankets, across patrolled borders in the middle of the night—accompanied by barking dogs that couldn't be shooed away. After they were safely across, in addition to the money they had agreed on, their Russian driver demanded certain cherished possessions they had planned to take to America. This booty, he claimed, was fair payment for the unforeseen risks he had taken along the way.

Not to be omitted from the family's epic saga, Uncle Harry and Dad could tell how they were separated from the rest of the family almost at the last moment by authorities who—discovering pockmarks on their scalps—insisted on sending them to Leipzig, Germany, to be quarantined for an undetermined time. Faced with this dilemma, my grandmother arranged for the rest of the family to board the ship and continue their journey to America while she and the boys went to Germany.

In Leipzig, the boys endured a series of harrowing examinations. Finally, it was decided their heads should be shaven and tarred, just to be safe. Their quarantine lasted three months, during which time new rumors circulated daily about the increasing numbers of families who were being rejected by inspectors, sometimes arbitrarily, because of a stringent effort by the United States to avoid contagious diseases from reaching its shores. Fortunately, at the end of the three months, they were allowed to proceed.

Meanwhile, my three aunts—and the two small cousins my grandmother brought with her from Russia—had been claimed by a contingent of New York relatives who were waiting for them at the dock near Ellis Island. The two little girls were taken directly to their prearranged destination, while Helen, Lillian, and Elsie went to New York to live with Ike's family until they could be reunited and continue their journey to Sioux City, Iowa, where Zayda waited in the apartment he had rented for them.

It was close to our bedtime now. Summing up the stories, Aunt Elsie said it was a miracle, but with God's help, everybody made it safely to America. America! She always said it ebulliently. She could recall every detail of the day they finally reached Ellis Island. She told us people began to gather along the rail long before there was anything to see. Then they began to point to a speck on the horizon. As the speck grew larger, she found a place underneath the rail between two men where she could see. She couldn't tell what everyone was looking at yet, but suddenly there it was, glittering in the sun, more beautiful than she thought it would be, her first sight of the Statue of Liberty and her welcoming torch. As it grew bigger, she could see a flotilla of small boats filled with waving people who were coming to meet the ship. They were shouting the first English word she ever heard, "Hello, Hello!" The words seemed to dance along on the water. She never saw anything so thrilling, she said. I think it was Aunt Elsie's pivotal moment.

The sky was now a black star-studded curtain. Moths, attracted by the light from the store window, hurled themselves into the glass, plummeting to the sidewalk, where they lay stunned, wriggling their useless legs.

It was time for bed. Single file, but pushing and shoving, we climbed the steps to the apartment above the store. When we were older, we were allowed to sleep at Uncle Harry and Aunt Ann's house across town. Then we pushed and shoved each other into the car, occupying any crack of space we could find. Turning around in the back seat, I watched our grandmother begin her slow, painful ascent up the stairs. Zayda, still stationed on the sidewalk, began to wave at our retreating car.

I waved back at him, watching him become smaller and smaller until his waving figure and the blinking fish disappeared into the still dark night.

Who knows why some families stay close for generations and some can't make it through one? Even after my grandparents died, the Schulmans remained a close and devoted family. Maybe it had something to do with their being an immigrant family, but I think it was nothing more complicated than the fact that they loved being together.

As long as my parents' generation stayed intact, we continued to get together regularly, although we modified the tradition to include an annual golf tournament. By then, our father's interest in golf had spread through the family to his siblings, his children, and his grandchildren. We named our tournament "The Schulman Open," and it grew more elaborate and more intergenerational with the passing years.

First, we added a traveling trophy and engraved the winner's name each year; then we included a banquet thrown by the previous year's winner—an idea we admittedly borrowed from the Master's Tournament, but we parsimoniously stopped short of bestowing green jackets.

A year or two later, we were forced to establish an adjunct tournament for the disgruntled relatives who were not invited to play with the "champions"—a loose and generous term—but who wanted to play nine holes and attend the banquet. This included the aunts, who took up golf in their seventies, as well as protesting in-laws and hangers-on. (Our reunions always seemed to attract friends of the family who wanted to be declared Schulmans on a temporary basis. It must have been the company or the food; it couldn't have been the golf.)

My favorite event of the tournament came the night before, which we began to call the "bargaining session." This was when we determined our handicaps for the tournament. It was an evening of cajoling and whining until we were satisfied we had been given the maximum number of strokes we could wheedle from all the others. During these evenings I discovered my true calling—dickering. Who knew?

As the only female in the "champions" group, I used this card and any others I thought I could get away with. During one of these sessions, Uncle Harry gave me a new nickname, "Little Big Mouth." Although he attended the event as eagerly as the rest of us, he was far too dignified and honorable to stoop as low as I was willing to do.

The bargaining event became very popular, even with the non-golfers, because of its reputation for raucous behavior. There were spirited catcalls, groans, and expressions unsuitable for framing. In the middle of one of these sessions, my mother suddenly took the floor and announced she was pulling for me. This was so astonishing I had to ask why. "Because you are running out of time," she pointed out, never one to pussyfoot around groping for diplomacy. But, as it turned out, time was running out for all of us.

Lillian and Elsie, now both widows, sold their houses in Detroit and New York and moved to Scottsdale, Arizona, where Helen and Abe had retired. Not since Petrikov had the three sisters actually lived in the same town. The golf tournament ended abruptly a few years later when Dad's Parkinson's disease advanced to the point where he couldn't play anymore. It wouldn't be a Schulman Open without him.

Our seniors were now all in their middle and late eighties, and traveling became too difficult for them. Scottsdale became the new family hub for a while, but time continued its relentless march. In the next few years, Mother and Dad moved to Houston—first to a facility offering a range of services from independent to assisted living, where they lived together briefly—then Dad to a nursing home and Mother to an apartment of her own. They were lost without each other at first, but Mother was making a good start on a new life when, suddenly, shockingly, she developed an aneurism and died.

Then Helen died. Our reunions now were cobbled

together for special occasions— Lillian's ninetieth birthday and later Elsie's. Elsie and Lillian made a smooth transition to life in Scottsdale after all those years in other places. They both moved into the Scottsdale Shadows, a lovely, sprawling community with amenities that included the nine-hole golf course where they learned to play. They had thought originally that they would live together, but soon found they had grown too independent and too dissimilar. Elsie joined the choir and took painting lessons; Lil found a good bridge game and read every book by a Jewish author she found in the library. Forced to become ecumenical, she moved on to Christian authors.

Unexpectedly, well into her eighties, Aunt Lil began to "see" (I am stumped for a verb here) a widower whose late wife had been Lil's bridge partner. He was the first man in Lillian's life for over fifty years. We watched her bloom—a still-blonde rose in that desert—until time caught up with them too. They were together for Lil's ninetieth birthday celebration and then, not long after, her special friend died.

Most of the Schulmans lived well into their nineties, healthy and active almost to the end. It is remarkable how much each of them accomplished in their lives with very little formal education. When they arrived here, since none of the children could speak or understand English, they were all placed in kindergarten. This was intolerable to Helen and Dad, the two oldest, who immediately quit school and went to work. I think the others graduated from high school.

Their formal education may have been limited, but they were equipped with formidable internal resources. They all grew into strong, highly evolved individuals, yet they remained a devoted family, leaving a very high standard for us, the next generation. When Harry, the last of them, died recently, we felt adrift. We had never known a time when they weren't part of our lives. As my brother Rick said, trying to express the magnitude of their contribution to our lives, "They taught us how to be Schulmans." And so they did.

When I think of them, as I often do, my trolling memory gets hooked on the fish market days when they were all in the fullness of life. In my mind's eye, I can see my father, uncle Harry, and Zayda, always somewhat competitive with each other, arguing over the correct way a prayer should be sung. Sitting around the dining room table, Helen, Lillian, and Elsie are absorbed in one of their projects, most of which ended up in our houses as hot pads, couch throws, aprons, or occasionally as competent oil or watercolor paintings. They are all inextricably woven into my sense of self, although I regret I inherited woefully few of their distinguishing characteristics.

Helen, the oldest, was a natural beauty. She had chestnut-colored hair and long eyelashes. Soon after she arrived in Sioux City, she went to work at Martin's Department Store. Hired as a "drummer" (someone who gathers a crowd to demonstrate new products), she was so petite and attractive that she was promptly promoted to modeling hats and shoes in Martin's tearoom.

She was very young when she married Abe Baker. They opened their first grocery store in Walnut, Iowa, followed by another in Avoca, and another in Harlan, until Baker's grew into a chain of supermarkets that blanketed metropolitan Omaha. Even after the family became millionaires, Helen continued to make a complete dinner for Abe every night, no matter what time he came home from the stores, which was often after midnight.

My favorite memories of her are the times my cousin Bob and I persuaded her to say our favorite Yiddish curse. Jewish curses are rarely eloquent or subtle; in fact, they are usually so convoluted they end up being more humorous than threatening: "You should have a large and well-stocked business and what you've got, nobody should ask for." Or, "You should burn up and be uninsured."

Spoken in Yiddish, they roll off the tongue in a satisfying and highly entertaining way, especially when articulated by Aunt Helen, who could never say the curse without dissolving into helpless laughter through which we could barely hear the words: "*Zolst vaksn vie a tsibele, mitn kop in dr'erd.*" In English this means, "May you grow like an onion, with your head in the ground." But, like so many Yiddish translations, you only get the words, not the flavor. It's impossible to do justice to this curse, because the word "onion" is boring vanilla compared to "*tsibele,*" which is like mocha almond fudge.

Everyone called Lillian, the middle sister, "Babe," which fit her perfectly. She seemed to skim along on the surface of life, kept buoyant by her generous and easy-going nature. Her husband, Sam Katz, a family favorite, had a truck and delivered newspapers in Detroit. He died young, leaving her with three small daughters to raise and very little money. Somehow she managed, with an occasional lift from the family, particularly Helen. Frugal by nature, she drew on her inherited ability to stretch a kopek. She saved and redeemed coupons from the Raleigh cigarettes she smoked and from the copious books of S & H Green Stamps collected for her by the entire family. (I remember many "licking" sessions when all of us were drafted.)

She may have been the very model of a walking serenity prayer, but this is not to say she wasn't spunky. Her favorite drink was Southern Comfort, a tangy 100-proof whiskey—and there was that elopement to Chicago to marry her husband, Sam, thus providing my grandmother, Hodel (or Odell), a.k.a. Ms. Keen, Tracer of Lost Persons, with another case. Come to think of it, how did my grandmother sniff out the exact whereabouts of her escaping children in the big city of Chicago? Who was the mole? I suspect Uncle Harry, but now there is no one to ask.

Physically, Aunt Lil looked different, too, as though an errant Viking gene had slipped into her inherited Ashkenazic gene pool. She was tall and blonde, with long shapely legs (a genetic gift passed along to only one of her three daughters). She outlived two of her daughters and died in her sleep just short of her ninety-sixth birthday—the gracious and painless death she deserved. From the delicious dishes that emerged from her kitchen, which we continue to make to this day, to the afghans she knitted for each of us— in all the right colors— to the many times she arrived on the doorsteps of her siblings whenever they needed her, her generosity brightened our lives.

Elsie, the youngest sister, was considered the creative one. She was the one I wanted to be like, because she could sing like Lily Pons and she had "golden hands." That's how the family described her. She could knit and sew beautifully, and she could design anything from wedding gowns to stunning suits. Who can forget the amazing reversible coat she made one year? Later, her golden hands designed and produced Braille books for blind children, which she "illustrated" with feathers, fabrics, and other tactile objects. Her creative juices followed her to Scottsdale, where she began to render her memories into charming watercolor scenes. I remember her scenes of the cobblestone streets of Petrikov, her colorful renderings of children ice-skating with colorful mittens and flying scarves, and, of course, the New York Harbor as she remembered seeing it that first time.

I loved all the stories about Elsie's childhood pursuits, especially the ones about her choreographic stage, during which she created elaborate routines, dancing along the tops of furniture which she pushed together, finally leaping off a dresser into the obliging arms of her admiring brother, Harry.

But my favorite Elsie memory doesn't have anything to do with her accomplishments. It happened the time she visited us in Oak Park, where my family lived just before I left for college. She had brought Alan, her young son then around three years old, with her. She was sitting on the floor of the downstairs guest bathroom observing Alan as he sat in the tub. He was soapy, his blonde curls damp from his wet washcloth.

As I walked past, I heard her say, "Alan, did you wash your penis?"

She said *penis*!

I couldn't believe it. No one in my family had ever used that word. Everyone tiptoed around it, using other "p" words like "puki" or "pee-pee," or even "privates."

But no one ever used the raw, unwrapped, hanging-out medical term. She was our only "emancipated woman"—until the next generation, when we came up with many "p" words that made "penis," like the word "onion," plain vanilla.

Elsie ended her days in an extended-care facility near her family in North Carolina. She attended a poetry reading the day before she died and was teaching her Irish-Catholic granddaughter a Yiddish song they planned to sing together. She had a project right to the end.

Ironically, she and Lillian died two months apart—almost to the day, dying as they lived, in sync. While they both lived in Scottsdale, they regularly attended Friday night services at the little synagogue they loved, where the congregation knew them as "the sisters." When they were well into their eighties, they undertook the extensive preparation required, and became bat mitzvah. They said they wanted to do it because it had been denied to women when they were growing up. I see this final undertaking as a symbol, not only of their life-long bond to Judaism, but also to each other.

Harry, the baby Schulman, having survived Elsie's terpsichorean period without emergency surgery, bulked up to became a stalwart competitor in our annual Schulman Open Golf Tournament. He was an amazing golfer. As my brothers point out, he could hit a drive three hundred yards and whiff the next one. His contributions to our family compendium of golf stories spark lively memories all these years later, particularly the time he sank an endless, downhill, sharply breaking putt on the eighteenth hole of the Davenport Country Club to snatch the tournament, and the trophy, right out of the waiting hands of my son, Jon.

But golf was not Harry's only talent. He was also Omaha's "Handy Man," the host of a popular radio show that ran for years. We all looked forward to his visits—not only for his amenable personality, but also because he left us with newly tightened knobs, properly hung pictures, functioning appliances, and a full drawer of unrecognizable tools he said we needed.

Anyone this estimable would naturally have no trouble attracting life companions. He had two. When his wife, Ann, died (another family candidate for sainthood and the mother of his two children), he found Sophie. It may be more accurate to say Ann found Sophie for him.

Sophie was an avid reader, intelligent, and a liberated feminist. I don't think my conservative uncle knew what hit him, but they were wonderful together. She was his companion through their eighties and into their nineties. Sophie died unexpectedly at the age of ninety-three, before she had a chance to read the last books I sent her: *Dancing on the Edge of the World: Jewish Stories of Love, Faith, and Inspiration*, and a mystery by her favorite writer, Rochelle Krich, the only one of the author's countless books she hadn't read.

Her death marked the end of independent living for Harry. He lived almost three years at the Remington Heights retirement home in Omaha. Lucky with women to the end, his daughter Estelle came to live with him there. She said she wanted to get to know him again after being away for over forty years. He died at ninety-five surrounded by family.

I haven't written much about my grandmother, Hodel, because I never really got to know her. She was far too busy working to pay much attention to me. All I know about her early life is that she was a twin and that her parents had sixteen children. I think most of them left Russia at around the same time, during the First World War. My grandmother came to the United States, one of her sisters went to South America, and the rest of the Hochmans ended up in what was then called Palestine.

My grandmother was a gritty and intrepid woman; I think she was in her sixties when she decided to fly to Israel (Zayda was afraid to go). It was her first trip in an airplane, and it was not a short journey, but she could not be dissuaded. She wanted to see her family once more, especially her twin. I know it was her first family reunion since Petrikov. I wish I had paid more attention to the details of her trip. It seems strange to realize there is no one left to ask.

Although there wasn't much interaction between my grandmother and me, I used to observe her silently as she moved heavily from one task to another. She had bad legs, yet several times a day she would make her way up and down the steep steps from the apartment to the store. In the morning, I often stood by her bed and watched her wind white strips of cloth tightly up her calves. She covered the strips with her thick stockings, securing it all with narrow elastic hoops above her knees.

Compared to the girth of her body, her legs were surprisingly thin and shapely, long fragile stems dangling from her round, apple body. Even more surprising was her long gray hair, which she braided and twisted into a severe bun at the back of her neck. I liked to follow her into the bathroom at night to see her pull out the tortoise hairpins and watch her hair cascade like a waterfall almost to her waist. I never tired of witnessing this magical transformation of my plain, hard-working grandmother into a storybook illustration.

She may have been the "meat and potatoes" of the family, the one who kept it all together, but it was Reb Mayer who gave our lives zest. Full of *Yiddishkeit* (Jewish culture), he had a piquant wit, which he used to spice his stories, throwing in clever asides and unexpected endings—an O. Henry of Jewish storytellers. My uncle Ray, who admired Zayda greatly, said Zayda's metaphors were verbal works of art.

I knew enough Yiddish to appreciate him, but he was unfathomable to my children. I once took them to visit their ninety-three-year-old great-grandfather in the nursing home where he lived until his death. Although he struggled to find the English words to offer his rich, Talmudic self to them, and they tried valiantly to understand, there was too much language and too much culture missing to connect the dots.

Reb Mayer had buried his beloved wife many years before. Always articulate, at her funeral he stood before her pine casket and delivered an oratory, eloquently thanking her for the beautiful life they had shared. He watched silently as her body was lowered into the ground. We all cried and thought her death would kill him, but a few years later, he announced his intention to marry again.

His children were shocked and disapproving, but they came to see he had accepted my grandmother's death as one of God's irrefutable decrees. He had loved her deeply, but like the fish that circled the cold metal tanks in his fish market, he was still swimming and full of life. He lived to bury his second wife, Sarah, too—but not before she succeeded in introducing him to the world of Miami Beach and mink stoles.

He adapted to life in the Jewish nursing home because he had to, but he made it more palatable for himself by assuming the position of "house maven." (He wasn't a *Kohayn*, a member of the tribe of priests, for nothing). The other residents accepted this with grace, and he remained unchallenged on such matters as how the holiday rituals should be observed. When he could, Dad would fly to Omaha from New Orleans and they would conduct High Holy Day services together. It was a gift to the residents, but perhaps even more, a gift to each other.

Zayda remained the house maven to the end. I will always be grateful to him for his ardor, his gusto, and, most of all, for his gift of laughter. I would like to feel that he lives on in all of us. Would he approve of what we have become? Some of us have divorced, some have intermarried, and some of us are not observant Jews. Still, I think he would take comfort in the fact that our Yiddishkeit persists, clinging like the sawdust on our shoes as we walked behind the counters of his fish market.

On the Road Again (without Willie Nelson)

"The road to success is always under construction."
—Lily Tomlin

I was raised when few books on raising children were written—not that anyone in my family would have bought one of those books. I don't think parents spent a lot of time thinking about their children's psyches in those days. They just lived their lives accompanied by their children.

Today you hear a lot about parenting "styles." I would be hard pressed to describe my parents' efforts on my behalf as a "style," unless there's a "flying by the seat of your pants" style. It was definitely not a "codependent" style. For example, if my parents decided it was time to move, we moved; even if these moves were taking place at tricky times for me, like halfway through a semester or three months before graduation from high school, for instance—both of which happened.

In cinematic terms, I would describe my early childhood as a road movie, but it didn't resemble the ones with Bob Hope, Bing Crosby, and Dorothy Lamour. We weren't moving to Tahiti or Zanzibar; we were moving within a small geographic area in Iowa whenever and wherever my father could find work: tending bar, hauling fish, driving a truck, clerking in a store. Later, I realized that we were among the millions of Americans who were also on the move trying to survive the Great Depression.

Not only wasn't it Tahiti or Zanzibar, it wasn't Dorothy Lamour in a colorful sarong aboard a glamorous ship. It was my mother in an old housedress, cooking and cleaning in a tiny dark apartment in Griswold, Iowa, and me under the table eating the cucumber slices she was planning to serve for lunch, thinking she would never suspect me if she didn't see me. Or it was my mother in an old housedress, cooking and cleaning in a tiny dark apartment in Avoca, Iowa, and me covered with my perpetual case of ringworm, which my mother said was caused by my insistence on petting all the neighborhood dogs and cats, despite her warnings. All of my childhood illnesses were diagnosed and treated by my multi-tasking mother, who practiced medicine (without benefit of a license) throughout her life, as her mother had before her. And they had the same two magic remedies for everything: cod liver oil and/or milk of magnesia.

I wish the script could segue now to my parents' impecunious but happy marriage, one resembling Ozzie and Harriet's, but such happiness was fragmentary for George and Anne. Introduced by mutual friends at a dance, they were immediately attracted to each other, and their elopement followed soon after. (This corroborates my friend Linda's theory that if you marry while you are in your dancing stage, you will marry a dancer. But what happens, I have always wondered, if you marry during your phallic stage?)

My parents did seem to have a lot in common. Both were born in Europe and immigrated with their mothers and siblings to the Midwest in the 1920s, both their fathers came first and worked for many years to earn the passage for their wives and children, both had strong mothers who kept their families together, and both were very attractive and wanted to be somewhere else.

Despite this apparent commonality, their personal differences grew more pronounced with the passing years. My father was headstrong, ambitious, and hard working. His determination to do things his own way, even as a child, was the stuff of legend—at least in his own family. His childhood exploits were still being related to us with great relish by his siblings when they were all well into their eighties. No doubt he was difficult, but I suspect these stories may have been embellished through the years. Could he really have burned down Minsk?

A formal photograph of my father as a young man presents a dashing image. We, his children, think of this as his "Al Capone" look. Always well groomed, he is wearing a hat, an elegant scarf, and the faint smile and steady gaze that were characteristic of him until later in life when Parkinson's stripped away these distinctions.

What my mother was like in those days is harder for me to imagine. A part of her remains a mystery to me even now. She was certainly accessible and warm, but there was also something unknowable about her, a secret door to herself that she kept closed. Obviously, she was petite and very pretty. Photographs of her taken before I was born reveal a small-boned, stylish woman with flashing dark eyes and a slightly provocative smile. In one memorable studio picture, she appears as an adventurous flapper, her brown hair marcelled in continuous waves, ending dramatically in comma-shaped spit curls draped along her cheeks. She seems stylish and full of life and yet—perhaps I imagine this—her eyes are solemn and reflect a trace of sadness even then.

I believe that my father was drawn to her liveliness and sense of adventure. He may have seen in her a kindred spirit. I'm sure my mother was attracted to my father's dark good looks. Adding to his appeal, he offered a chance to escape the rancor leveled at her beloved father by her ambitious and frustrated mother. (I used to think it was ironic that you could grow up with hostility and then repeat it in your own marriage, but now I know it often happens that way.)

My mother was just sixteen when she eloped with my father. He was five years older, although this interval, unsubstantiated by official birth certificates, grew hazier with time and could contract or expand depending on who was counting.

When I was sixteen, it seemed incredible to me that my mother, who was anything but daring in my opinion, had actually run off at my same age to marry my father, a virtual stranger. I couldn't imagine taking on such responsibility or cutting myself off from the endless possibilities that could be my future. But, of course, the same endless possibilities didn't exist back then for either of them. And, as it turned out, I followed in her footsteps, although I was three years older than she was when I married.

Mother was eighteen when I was born, but the births of my three siblings took place over a more leisurely period of sixteen years. We aren't sure whether our parents were following the fashion of the day to have one child in school before the next one was born or if it was just the way it happened. In my opinion, it was another example of their seat-of-the-pants lifestyle. Because of these long fallow periods between gestations, my siblings and I have a whole different set of memories, and at times it has seemed we had totally different parents.

As the oldest, I have more memories of our parents' early years together. This is both good and bad news. Because there was more heat between them back then, I probably saw more displays of affection, but their outbursts may have been more rancorous. I'm not sure what my parents argued about in those days. Either I have successfully suppressed these memories, or I managed to block them out by closing my bedroom door and burying my head under a pillow to wait out the storm. Although these storms began to subside more quickly over the years, I suspect that the gap between them grew larger.

I can only speculate about what went wrong, because by the time I was old enough to ask them about it, I was trying to distance myself from the whole thing and accept it all as just the way it was. I probably didn't want to know more because I was protecting my fragile neutrality in the ongoing battle.

Not that things were relentlessly bleak; there were good times when they were able to rekindle the spark. They chose to live together the rest of their lives—over sixty years—and I believe something more than their four children held them together. Faded photographs in an old album substantiate this belief. There is one of my smiling parents on a fishing trip, proudly displaying their catch; in another they are clowning with friends in the back of a pickup truck. A later album shows them elegantly dressed for a night on the town, my father's arm around my mother, and on the same page my mother appears as a blonde siren, her hair swept into fashionable curls, sitting at a bar, surrounded by men, including my father—he, just one of the smiling, admiring crowd.

I remember extended periods in various apartments when, if not Ozzie and Harriett, my parents seemed gay and carefree with each other. They had totally different philosophies about money, and I know this was an ongoing issue, but if we were poor I didn't know it. There always seemed to be money for extras, like tap-dancing lessons. Later, a small spinet piano appeared, ushering in weekly piano lessons. A growing pile of yellow music books from the Charles Scribner Library accompanied these lessons. Unfortunately, they featured scales and fingering assignments, which I ignored because they ruined everything.

Since our moves never seemed to occur at the end or the beginning of a semester and often took us to a different town, each of these moves meant a new school for me. Inevitably, the new class was studying something unfamiliar and often using a different book. This meant I was an outsider again, a stranger who didn't know the answer to any question. It became clear to me early on that I had to find a way to fit in or go through life as a loner.

I'm not sure how I did it, but eventually, one relationship following another, I finally mastered "ingratiation skills," and my life definitely improved. With our move to Sioux City, Iowa, I moved from the wings of life to center stage—literally. Show business beckoned during my first week in Floyd School when my teacher went up and down the aisles of my classroom, her hand cupped around her ear, listening to us vocalize. Then she stood at the front of the room and announced the names of the students she had chosen to represent our class at a special assembly for parents. My song was "Carry Me Back to Old Virginny." For this performance, I appeared in blackface, dressed in a long, flowered pinafore with a bandanna tied around my head. (This program obviously preceded the concept of political correctness.)

The event is memorable because it is the only time I can remember my mother coming to a school program. It is also memorable because my disguise did not fool my sharp-eyed, three-year-old brother, Ron, who accompanied her. Never one to consider the subtleties of possible embarrassment to his older sister—then or later—he screeched, "That's Donnie!"

Following this toehold into show biz, a year or two later I was chosen to play Mary in the Christmas play. (As the only Jewish child in that entire school, what were they thinking?) Mary could be considered a leading role, but since this was a pageant, Mary had no lines. My only job was to hold the baby Jesus in a basket on my lap and look enraptured. My rapture was illuminated by a light bulb buried along the side of the baby's blanket, which was focused on my face. Halfway through the production, baby Jesus began to smoke; soon a hole burned through the blanket. I managed to dig around in the basket, redirect the lamp, and remain enraptured until the curtain closed.

Despite this display of courage—and my commitment to the principle of "the show must go on,"—that was the end of my acting career until high school. It was just as well, because my mother wasn't too crazy about my developing a long-term relationship with the baby Jesus. This was the first time the subject of my being Jewish was ever mentioned, and it was a genuine surprise to me. My earlier exposure to my grandparents' religious practices only meant that *they* were Jewish. Since we didn't light candles or recite Hebrew prayers or eat brisket or chicken on Friday night, how was I to know?

Discovering that I wasn't like everyone else in my class was very bad news. Besides, I had already memorized all the Christmas carols, and I liked singing them. Especially "The Twelve Days of Christmas," which I had memorized from "a partridge in a pear tree" through "twelve drummers drumming." Now my mother was telling me we didn't believe in Jesus. That is, we believed he was a nice man, but not the part about his being God's son. For that reason, she said, it would be better if I didn't sing Christmas songs. What a waste!

Not long after this conversation, a big yellow bus with a six-pointed star came to pick me up several afternoons a week after school. Mastering Ray's entire bar mitzvah when I was five apparently was not good enough. Now I had to go to Hebrew school and learn to read and understand Hebrew. Why? Couldn't I just pray in English?

But things were about to get worse.

After surviving the Jesus trauma and managing to entrench myself in the flourishing social milieu of Floyd School in Sioux City—as demonstrated by receiving a Valentine's Day card from everyone in the class—I learned that my parents were going about to ruin my life by moving us again. This time we were moving to

Chicago, where I was sure to be an outsider again, because I would be living in a much bigger city with much bigger schools.

They were heartless! They were making me leave my extended family and all my friends. Herbert Borofsky would no longer crawl under his parents' bed to call me on school nights when his parents went out. Lucia Augustine and Beverly Benson wouldn't be my best friends any more. Mother wouldn't take me shopping and buy me BLT sandwiches at Martin's Department store.

I cried hysterically, but we moved anyway.

My Vacation in Walnut

"You don't have to suffer to be a poet; adolescence is enough suffering for anyone."
—John Ciardi

The summer I was twelve, my parents announced I would be going to Walnut, Iowa, to spend a week or so in the country with the Bakers: Aunt Helen, Uncle Abe, and their sons, Bob and Jack. (Debbie, the daughter Aunt Helen longed for, didn't make her appearance until much later, when it was practically too late for her to show up.)

This announcement surprised me. I had never traveled anywhere without my parents, and nobody had even asked me if I wanted to go. I don't know why this should have surprised me. Have I mentioned that parenting in my family was not democratic? The governing construct in my family was very efficient, because power was concentrated in very few hands, mostly my father's. It was like being raised by António Salazar or Mustafa Kemal Atatürk or some other benevolent despot.

But I was happy about this particular decree. Bob was my favorite cousin, and I had never been in the "country" before. I imagined streets filled with horses and tractors, if they had streets, and me feeding chickens and gathering eggs every day. I didn't imagine that I would be making a developmental leap while I was there, but my transitions have rarely announced themselves beforehand. I'm lucky to be able to recognize them after they happen. "Leap," in my case is definitely an overstatement; "hop" might be better.

I'm not sure how or why these arrangements were made, but since the whole family knew we were moving to Chicago by then, it was possible that Aunt Helen felt sorry for me because I was going to have to grow up on concrete. It's also possible that Aunt Helen just wanted the chance to get me out of braids. She told my mother once that I look like a skinned rabbit in them. Another time she told my mother that I should have at least one dress and a pair of dress shoes. Although Aunt Helen had very little experience in converting a "tomboy" into "a girly girl," a few days into my visit I began to suspect she was attempting a major makeover.

As we drove into Walnut, I could see I didn't have to worry about getting lost. The main business street was one or two blocks long, with stores and businesses lined up neatly on either side. Some of these places even had hitching posts in front of them, but no horses were tethered to them. Uncle Abe's store, Baker's, was in the middle of everything. As I remember it, the hardware store, the drug store, and the seed store were across the street, and the movie theater was a block away.

It was my plan to observe nature whenever I could on this vacation, because nature might be hard to find once we moved to Chicago. I remembered that my science teacher once told me nature hated a vacuum. I looked for evidence of this as we drove by a vacant lot between two buildings. From the car window, I could see weeds were growing over the cans and bottles that had been thrown on the ground there. Was that what she meant? Was nature trying to bury that trash under mounds the way Indians buried their dead? What about the whiskey and tobacco ads that were peeling down the brick walls in colorful ribbons? What was nature doing there—making a maypole?

The houses we passed—white or grey, some with pillars, others with porches—could be found anywhere, but the yards definitely looked "country." Swings made from rubber tires hung from the limbs of trees, and overalls and towels suspended from clotheslines flapped in the wind. Under the gutters of some houses were big barrels that Aunt Helen called rain barrels. She said people liked to use rainwater to clean tools, to water plants, and, especially, to wash everyone's hair because the water was soft and left your hair shiny and untangled. This was a clear example of nature at work. It rained in Chicago too—if we couldn't have a barrel there, could we have a big pan?

The Bakers' house was set back from the road on a grassy knoll. Aunt Helen pulled into the driveway, and I carried my suitcase into the cool front hall. It was empty except for a basket of music rolls and a player piano. A player piano was different from a plain piano. With a player piano you didn't have to wind anything or know anything to make real music. You just put a roll of paper with holes punched in it into slots on the piano. Then you could sit in a chair, pump the petals on the floor, and watch the holes make music just by moving across the page.

The Bakers' house had many rooms, but some, I was to learn, were rarely used. The room next to the hall that Aunt Helen called the "front room," for example, was used only when they had company, which never happened while I was there. There was also a formal dining room, complete with a buffet and a long, formal table with matching chairs, where no one ate. After I picked up the bowl of nuts that was always sitting in the middle of the table and found a hundred dollar bill stuck to the bottom of it, I learned that the dining room table's only purpose was to give Uncle Abe a place to spread out and count the money from the store's cash register every night.

Between the front room and the dining room was a cheerful room full of windows that overlooked the tree-lined side yard. This was the room the family used on the few occasions when they weren't working. All the furniture in this room was covered with the same blue nautical upholstery. The wooden arms of the couch and chairs were round, with spokes that connected to a wooden hub. I guessed they were meant to resemble steering wheels on a boat. A large console radio that said "Philco" stood along one wall. When Uncle Abe turned on the radio, the dial lighted up and crackling sounds accompanied the voice that could be heard through the fabric-covered panels along the front.

We ate all our meals in the kitchen. It was a big, pleasant room, but the only thing I remember about it is the pump sunk right into the counter next to the sink. It may have conveyed water from a well into the house for a specific purpose, but I didn't ask anyone about it, in case it was dumb for me not to know why it was there. I pumped the handle up and down to watch the water flow into a glass occasionally, but it was so much easier to get water from the faucet, the novelty soon wore off.

My room, off the kitchen, was a concrete slab with three walls of screens, connected to a section of the house's exterior. It was just big enough for a bed and dresser. I unpacked my suitcase quickly, pushed open the screen door, and went to look for Bob. Aunt Helen said I would probably find him near something she called the "pigeon coop." When I found him, he was with another boy. As I approached, the boys turned to look at me and immediately stopped talking. Breaking the awkward silence, Bob nodded toward his friend. "His name is Lawrence Weber," he said, adding, "She's my cousin."

After we acknowledged each other with nods, another awkward silence followed, now accompanied by shuffling feet.

"What do you want to do?" Bob asked me. "Do you want to see my pigeons?"

We walked around the garage to a chicken-wire shed filled with fluttering birds. As we approached, the birds began to squawk, flying from one perch to another. Bob opened the door and we walked inside.

Grabbing some corn from a feeder near the door, Bob offered it to a pigeon with a white head and black wings sitting on a nest of twigs. "This one's a nun," Bob said, like a guide in a museum. "She's nesting. Over there is her mate," he said, pointing to a matching pigeon. "After a while, he'll sit on the nest so she can take a rest. Pigeons mate for life, did you know that?"

Bob spoke with authority. He pointed to another bird. "That one, with the puffed up chest, is a pouter. The rest are mostly homers."

I was amazed at this sudden erudite flow of information. When had he learned all that?

"C'mon," said Lawrence Weber, poking the toe of his shoe into the chicken wire. "Let's do something. Did you ever shoot a BB gun?"

I shook my head. I didn't tell him I had never even seen a BB gun.

We walked down two or three houses to the Weber house. In his backyard near the alley, several tin cans had been soldered to the posts of a wire fence. Lawrence produced his prized Daisy Red Ryder BB gun from his garage, and we took turns trying to hit the cans.

That afternoon I learned about lowering your expectations. When I saw I wasn't going to hit a can, I contented myself with not flinching at the gun's recoil and making sure I didn't shoot myself or anybody else.

The days of my country vacation blended into a tapestry of sunny afternoons and warm, starry nights. I grew brown and freckled, and I squeezed in all the country things I could in my remaining days. I milked a cow once, and several times I went down the road to a neighbor's farm to gather fresh brown eggs for Aunt

Helen. I drank milk that wasn't pasteurized, and I washed my hair in the silky water from the rain barrel along the side of the house.

Whenever the movie changed, Bob and I walked to town. We were careful not to walk under the box elder trees. Box elder bugs could drop from the tree and dive-bomb down the back of your neck. We learned this the hard way. One night, as we walked to the movie, Bob suddenly took off down the street, screaming. Pulling up his shirt as he ran, I saw the orange-edged wings of a box elder bug fly out and disappear. After that, we walked along the curb.

If we had a long wait before the movie started, we would hang around Baker's. Bob usually got recruited to bag groceries, while I luxuriated at Uncle Abe's desk, busily snooping through his drawers. Once I found a box labeled "bust developer." I was very interested in what might be in the box because nothing was developing on me yet, but the only thing in it was a giant rubber band.

I tried to avoid going to the movies if it happened to be "bank night." Bank nights were held once a week all over the country during the Great Depression. They were initiated by the movie industry to entice the public to spend their money on a frivolity—like a movie. People were seduced by the prospect of winning a prize, usually pots and pans or dishes. These bank nights were supposed to be morale builders. They may not have boosted the spirits of the general public, but they definitely boosted the morale of the movie industry, which later credited bank nights with saving them.

The reason I hated to go on bank night was because, between movies, the manager would wheel a big glass cylinder filled with ticket stubs onto the stage. Turning the handle of the cylinder to rotate the stubs, he would choose someone from the audience to come up, draw a stub from the cylinder, and read the number printed on it. The person with the matching stub was the winner. After the winner's number was verified, he or she could redeem the prize.

Despite the bravado I displayed in my theatrical period, I was now going through a "shrinking violet" stage. My heart would start to pound at the sight of the glass cylinder, whereupon I would slink down in my seat and count the cracks in the concrete floor until the danger was over. If Bob ever noticed my cringing, he never mentioned it.

At some point during that vacation, Aunt Helen took me shopping. I think she felt it was time for my transformation because she drove me to Avoca, a bigger town than Walnut, with more stores. In one store she bought me a dress, in another she bought me a pair of dressy white shoes that buckled across the instep. I loved those shoes so much I didn't tell her how painful they were within seconds of wearing them.

A couple of days later, Aunt Helen told me to put on my new dress and the new shoes. As we walked to her neighbor's house I tried desperately not to limp. My toes, squeezed together like sardines in a can, were throbbing with pain by the time we rang the doorbell. Inside the neighbor's house, in a room similar to Aunt Helen's front room, I found two girls dressed the way I was, sitting stiffly in chairs. We drank lemonade and ate cookies and tried to find something to say to each other, but whatever Aunt Helen had in mind didn't happen. At least, not the way she had planned. If she was hoping to connect me to my latent inner girl-ness, she needn't have bothered. Nature was already on the job. I walked home carrying my shoes.

Toward the end of my vacation, I grew listless and bored. To Bob's disgust, I didn't feel like doing anything. All I wanted to do was stay home and read. I was tired of shooting tin cans; I had even lost interest in the pigeons. After he went off with his friends for the day, I sprawled on the glider in the side yard, reading and brooding.

One lazy afternoon, I thought I heard a horse trotting up the driveway. Peeking furtively around my book, I saw it was Bob's friend, Jack Wolfe, sitting on a reddish-brown horse. He had been over a few times, but we had never talked to each other. I thought he might be older than the other boys because he didn't clown around as much. I hoped he wouldn't notice me in the glider, but I could feel him looking my way. I put down my book and walked toward him.

"Hi," he said, as I approached. "Is Bob home?"

I shook my head. "I think he might be at the store."

He looked down at me with unwavering blue eyes. I looked up at him with quavering brown ones. I noticed the way he sat on his horse—confidently, the way cowboys do in westerns. I wondered if he practiced that in front of a mirror, the way I practiced lifting one eyebrow like Joan Crawford.

It was Jack Wolfe who broke the silence. "This is my

new horse," he said. "I came over to let Bob see it. I was going to take Bob for a ride. Would you like to go?"

I patted the house, stalling.

"I'd like to go," I said finally, deciding to be honest, "but I don't know anything about horses. I don't even know how to get up on one."

"Put your left foot in the stirrup," he directed. He reached down and lifted me unto the horse in front of him, reaching around me for the reins. Then he turned the horse around and steered him down the driveway. When we reached the road, he let the horse trot. I could feel the horse's bristly coat under my thighs. We were going faster now. The streets of Walnut whizzed by, concrete gave way to gravel and then to dirt. We were heading toward the open country. I let my body relax. I felt I was flying right into the future. Despite an exhilarating sense of freedom, I had an accompanying feeling of loss. I didn't realize then it was just another example of nature on the job.

My feeling of loss didn't last long. Life continued to be an exciting ride for both Bob and me. Despite Aunt Helen's fear that we would marry each other and produce imbeciles, we married other people and raised fairly normal children.

We don't see each other much anymore, but we try to keep in touch. We still have that deep connection you have for someone when you grow up together—and when you have practiced kissing each other, getting ready for the real thing.

I don't know what happened to Jack Wolfe, but Bob

told me recently that Lawrence Weber became a doctor. That's all he knows about him, because after Lawrence shot one of Bob's best carrier pigeons with his BB gun, Bob shot Lawrence with his, and that pretty much terminated their relationship.

After that summer, the future I was destined for changed from horses to boys, during which I put those early practice sessions with Bob to good use. As for Bob, he gave up his dream of being a doctor and ended up helping to build Baker's into the successful chain of supermarkets they became. He also gave up collecting pigeons and graduated to collecting classic Ferraris.

Life on Belmont Avenue

"I think that's how Chicago got started. A
bunch of people in New York said,
'Gee, I'm enjoying the crime and the poverty,
but it isn't cold enough. Let's go west.'"
—Richard Jeni

With our move to Chicago, I knew I wasn't going to be a big frog in a little pond anymore. I was going to be an amoeba in Lake Michigan. Our new apartment was on Belmont Avenue, just off Lake Michigan, on Chicago's North Side. When I saw that apartment, I stopped sniveling.

It was nothing less than a consciousness-raising event for me. I had no idea that apartments didn't have to be small and dark and plain. They could have amenities—fireplaces, butler's pantries, huge rooms, built-in shelves, spectacular views! Our new place had all those things.

I was given the front bedroom, and once I learned to balance myself while standing on the windowsill, I could see the boats bobbing in Belmont Harbor, especially on a clear, sunny day. The living room just overlooked Belmont, but it was enormous, and it had a real fireplace.

The dining room was even bigger than the living room, and along the wall next to the kitchen, there was a small room with lots of shelves that Mother called a butler's pantry (unfortunately, it didn't include the butler). I began to see that living in Chicago might offer some redeeming compensations.

In addition to our luxurious apartment, there was a girl about my age living in the apartment next door. Not long after we moved in, she invited me over to listen to her records. She had a bookshelf full of them, and her record player could play records by just clicking a switch. As we listened to music, we sat on the floor together and read the record covers.

That afternoon, I heard "That's America to Me," sung by Paul Robeson. I remember it distinctly because it didn't sound like any song I ever heard. While I listened, I looked at his picture on the cover. He seemed to be staring right back at me with big, soulful eyes. I don't remember the lyrics of the song, but his voice was unforgettable; it was pitched so low it seemed to reverberate in the room, and he knew how to make his words bite right into you.

I was still exploring the neighborhood when my parents announced we were moving again. I couldn't believe it. What was wrong with those people? As our moving day approached, I began to experience separation anxiety. I was sure that next place wouldn't be as grand as this one, and I was right.

The new apartment was still located on Belmont, but it was much farther away from Belmont Harbor. We were now just half a block from a major thoroughfare called Broadway. A variety of stores occupied both sides of the busy street. I remember a restaurant with a big window that displayed tantalizing ribs barbequing on a big rotating rack. A few doors down and across the street, a chicken store bragged, "Our Chickens Never Touch the Ground." (What was so good about that?) There was even a movie theater around the corner and a newsstand that sold Sunday's newspaper on Saturday night.

But no amount of gymnastics could produce a view of Lake Michigan or Belmont Harbor. Besides, this apartment had no amenities. It didn't have a fireplace or a butler's pantry, and—much worse—it didn't have a separate bedroom for me. As a budding adolescent with the outlandish privacy needs so typical of the age, I now had to share a bedroom with my little brother, the one who embarrassed me in the school program and who, by now, had developed into a real *nudge* (pest). His major purpose in life these days seemed to be spying on me and reporting my activities to our parents. If he had kept it up, he might have become J. Edgar Hoover, but even he could see that my life was not worthy of his observational efforts, and he moved on.

Our apartment was in an unembellished U-shaped brown brick building with a narrow courtyard between the wings. The wings were mirror images of each other, which meant we could look directly into the bedroom windows of the apartment across from us, and they could look directly into ours. Whenever I rolled up our window shades, I seemed to be looking right into the eyes of the boy who lived across from us. I complained about this to my mother, but she did not see this as a subject worthy of a discussion.

"So, keep your shades down," she said briskly, "and crawl around on your knees when you're getting dressed."

The case was closed. To my mother, this wasn't even a problem. A problem was something real, something that could be addressed with cod liver oil or milk of magnesia. We kept our shades down. I even undressed in the closet because of the potential peeping Tom occupying the twin bed next to mine.

Like most apartment buildings in our neighborhood, we had an entrance hall. This may be too grand a descriptor for the small vestibule just inside our front door. Brass mailboxes on both sides of the narrow space led to a glass door and the stairs to the apartments just beyond. Visitors—or me, if I forgot my key—could push the button above our mailbox, and someone in the apartment would buzz them in. It required a quick sprint to get to the glass door when the buzzer rang, because if the buzzer stopped before the door was opened, you were back to zero, pushing the button above our mailbox.

There were six apartments in our building, two to a floor. We were on the second floor, just below Howard, who played jazz piano day and night. The music wasn't bad, but Howard had developed the habit of accompanying himself by thumping—some would call it stomping—on the floor, which was not carpeted. I never talked to Howard about his ambitions, but if his goal was to get to Carnegie Hall, he was on the right track.

After a few weeks of traipsing up and down the steps, I realized that all six doors in our building had *mezuzahs* (parchment prayers rolled into a container and nailed to the doorframe). After another few weeks, I realized practically everyone in our neighborhood was Jewish. Was this a coincidence or a parental strategy?

However it happened, our move to Chicago was a

seminal event. My father's job with Morris Fisheries, the reason we moved there, was his introduction to corporate life and led to other opportunities. As for Mother, I believe her Chicago years were her halcyon days. She loved living in a big, modern city with so much to do, and she was motivated to participate in it all. The fact that Vicki was born while we lived in this apartment might have inspired her. Every nice day, Mother wrapped her in a blanket, put her in the buggy, and walked down to Belmont Harbor, where she met a collection of women who became her good friends. Sitting on benches, they talked and shared confidences, gently rocking their babies, who napped contentedly in the swarm of buggies and strollers.

Another important reason for her happiness was that there was more money now. For the first time in her life, Mother hired a cleaning lady, who came twice a week, giving her two afternoons of freedom. She used those afternoons in part to accomplish the absorbing mission of furnishing our apartment, for which my father, uncharacteristically, had given her a liberal budget and no interference.

With such freedom, it could be predicted that Mother would go modern with a vengeance. For a woman seemingly moderate in her convictions, my mother had a passionate, even philosophic position about being *au courant.* With her, it wasn't a matter of being fashionable or trendy, it was about being progressive. She welcomed fresh new ideas and innovation. Anything dark and old-fashioned depressed her. (She eventually tired of modern, at which point she moved on to "timeless simplicity," thus launching her oriental period, which she never outgrew.)

Since our living room in the Belmont apartment lacked

a focal point, she bought one: a glass-top table secured by three wooden legs, painted and carved to resemble feathers that joined at the bottom in a ring of pale brown wood, her favorite finish. Everything in our living room, except for my spinet piano, a hangover from our Sioux City days, was finished in that same, Scandinavian-inspired finish, known at the time as "blonde."

She bought a light beige sofa bed for the small sunroom off the living room—maybe nothing on which to focus, but something useful enough to accompany us on many future moves. (After she appeared, the sunroom became Vicki's bedroom. Was this event an example of my parents' "let's wing it" approach to family planning? If so, this was not going to be the last example of it.)

Mother went all out in the dining room, perhaps too far out. Once the buffet and the oval table with eight chairs were placed in the room, walking around in there was restricted to narrow paths between obstacles. This proved to be insignificant, because we ate all our meals on a chrome table in the kitchen anyway. The dining room was strictly for company, and since we rarely entertained at home, it quickly became the stage for her regular poker game. On these occasions, the table pads were reversed to their plush green side and poker chips, ashtrays, and bowls of candy and nuts fought for space along the edges of the table. (Mother played all games well. In Omaha, with her brothers, it was spirited hands of gin rummy; in Sioux City, it was mah-jongg, popular with Chinese men and Jewish women [rarely played together]; in Chicago, it was poker; later, in New Orleans, it was bridge.)

When the poker game was at our house, after school I might find her seated at the head of the dining room table in a haze of smoke surrounded by her friends. The usually silent dining room then resembled a state of siege, invaded by boisterous and unintelligible conversation, occasionally interrupted by shrieks of laughter.

If Mother's cards had been bad that afternoon, I might see a quarter affixed to her forehead, which she hoped would change her luck. I usually hung around until it was her turn to deal the cards because it was an amazing spectacle, akin to watching Dr. Jekyll turn into Mr. Hyde. Shedding her normally subdued demeanor, my mother dealt cards with the aplomb of a shill while delivering a wry commentary on the visible potential each hand. This intriguing glimpse of my mother revealed a facet of her that only appeared on these occasions.

We lived in our apartment on Belmont from my last year in grammar school through most of my high school life. During this interval, Mother hit her social peak. She became a blonde and then a redhead. She learned where to shop for designer clothes at discount prices. She wore handsome cocktail suits and elegant platform shoes. She was definitely *au courant*.

Meanwhile, my father was also polishing his rough edges. Having witnessed the lifestyles of the upper echelon of his company, some of whom lived along Chicago's North Shore, he began to wear custom-made suits and hand-painted ties. He bought season tickets for the Chicago Blackhawks and took us to hockey games. Later, he joined Tam O'Shanter Country Club, the home of what was called the "All American Open Golf Tournament."

Is there an "acculturation" stage during which the children of immigrants enthusiastically embrace the middle-class Anglo-Saxon value system of their host country? If so, that was my parents' stage at this time. As their cultural awareness grew, they began to shed their provincial skins. They looked authentic on the outside, but they never really transformed themselves into North Side Chicago Jews. It took the next generation to do that.

My entry into city life was not as smooth as that of my parents. Although Nettelhorst, my new grammar school, was just a short walk along Broadway, it could have been on another continent as far as I was concerned. Every morning, I trudged off to school alone, except for the honking cars, clanging streetcars, babies in strollers, and kids on bicycles.

Nettelhorst looked as sinister as its name. An old, red-brick building with chunks of missing mortar and a heavy metal door sunk into a stone entrance, it looked more like a prison than a school. In Iowa, my school had been small and modern, with bright red and yellow displays of student projects in every window and a grassy schoolyard. Nettelhorst had bars on the windows and it was surrounded by concrete and gravel.

The school was different on the inside too. Instead of cheerfully painted cloakrooms at the back of the classroom where you could put your things, Nettelhorst had chipped and scratched metal lockers along the building's halls. As for the textbooks and the assignments, it was hopeless. As I had feared, my class was using a different textbook, and the assignments were way ahead of what we had been studying in my old school.

Even the teachers were different. They seemed so

remote and unapproachable I was afraid to ask them to explain anything. The worst thing was, my ingratiation skills were not working here. My classmates, together since kindergarten, were a cohesive group who had absolutely no interest in me. I wasn't interested in them, either. I thought they were rude. No one waited to be called on here. They eagerly volunteered to answer every question the teacher asked, sometimes before she asked it. Their hands were up constantly, and they never stopped talking. After a week or so, I gave up wanting to fit in.

I hated everybody, particularly my parents. It was their fault. I realized by now that our living in this primarily Jewish neighborhood wasn't a coincidence. One clue was that my mother, who had never expressed an interest in my friends before, suddenly wanted to know all about my classmates. What were they like, she asked? What were their names?

Finally she stopped pussyfooting around and said that she and Dad thought it was time for me to make some Jewish friends—not exclusively, she said, just some. Apparently giving up Jesus and being able to read Hebrew were still not enough for her.

Much later, when I came to understand the socioeconomic makeup of our neighborhood, I grasped that we were living in an ecosystem with an invisible yet discernable hierarchy. This was worse than being an outsider, now I was a member of the lowest level of biological organization you still could consider living; I was scraping along like a catfish, in the "bottom feeder" phylum.

In the socioeconomic world in which we were living, what you wore and where you lived could define you. Our own neighborhood was a good example. If you lived on the other side of Broadway you were in one classification. If you lived on our side, you were in another. Two blocks closer to the lake, in one of the high-rise buildings along Lake Shore Drive, you were at the top.

Sometimes you get lucky and fate intervenes to solve your stickiest problem; that's what happened to me. Through no machination of my own, one of the boys in my class, Ronny Samuels, was having a bar mitzvah, and his parents invited all the Jewish children in the class to attend it, including me.

This whole Jewish thing was still mystifying to me: How did Ronny Samuels's parents know I was Jewish? Why was it important to have Jewish friends? Did being Jewish change your whole life? My mother received my invitation to the bar mitzvah with the same enthusiasm she had displayed in embellishing our apartment, only now she was embellishing me. She insisted that I needed an appropriate new outfit to wear. Normally, my father was of the opinion that one outfit in your life should be enough, but for once he agreed without argument.

My new outfit was a gray pinstriped suit selected by my father's Irish secretary, Bernadette, who took me shopping and must have attended a bar mitzvah in Ireland, because her choice was so appropriate that one of my classmates turned up in the same suit. I don't think it was the suit, but that turning point in Ronny Samuels's life became a turning point in mine.

Not long after the bar mitzvah, Natalie Harris, one of the most popular girls in my class and definitely the smartest one, actually took on the thankless task of being my first Jewish friend. Sadly, shortly after his thirteenth birthday, Ronny Samuels, the friendly chubby boy with the horn-rimmed glasses and happy disposition who made all this possible, died of spinal meningitis. Until then, I didn't realize that children could die. I went to the funeral with my classmates, but I couldn't think of a way to tell his parents that their invitation to Ronny's bar mitzvah changed my life. How could I, when their lives had changed so tragically?

By the time I reached high school, I knew how to traverse Sandburg's "brawling, big shouldered" Chicago by myself. I frequently took the double-decker buses to Michigan Avenue and to the Loop. I was also familiar with the elevated trains, known as the El, which went places the buses didn't. I could find the public library, the Art Institute, and Marshall Field's, including all the departments that carried my size.

On Saturdays, I walked to the Century Theater on Diversey with my friends, all of whom lived within blocks of our apartment and represented the whole spectrum of our socioeconomic universe, to see the latest movie. After the movies, we either went for chicken potpies at O'Connell's or we bought hot dogs from one of the vendors along Lake Shore Drive. It's difficult to describe the delights of a Chicago hot dog to the uninitiated, especially the hot dogs bought from a vendor on the street. There is just something about the pop of the hot dog, onions cascading down the front of your clean white blouse, yellow mustard crusting on your upper lip, that cannot be conveyed. As Hannah Arendt once said—not about hot dogs—"Words can never convey the pleasure of an experience."

Not only was I familiar with all this, I totally

understood the pervasive caste system of Chicago's North Side, as delineated by Nicholas Senn High School, where this knowledge was crucial. It took only a quick orientation to tell the players, particularly the girls. The "stars," the urbane offspring living along or near the Drive, wore Pringle cashmere sweaters and the long "New Look" skirts, which grazed their ankles. Many of them also wore "Dr. Becker" noses, recognizable by a certain sculptured flair of the nostrils. And, of course, they belonged to the right sororities and fraternities. Or maybe it was the other way around: because they belonged to them, they became the right sororities and fraternities.

In case you think I am making this up or exaggerating see Joseph Epstein's book *Snobbery: The American Version*. He also went to Senn—where, he observes, "Status was at least as carefully calibrated as at the court of the Sun King at Versailles." With so much riding on this status symbol, we all felt a tremendous pressure to "rush." Rushing was the arduous screening process you had to undergo before you were accepted into one of these groups. I knew it would be painful, but in the mindless way you want everything your cohort wants when you are a teenager, I was willing to subject myself to immolation if my friends were doing it. At fifteen, the drive for popularity may equal the drive for survival.

You couldn't be member of a sorority just by wanting to be one; you had to receive invitations to three interminable teas, where you actually drank tea, munched cookies, and made small talk with the members, knowing that while you were subjecting yourself to this seemingly innocuous process, you might inadvertently fail some covert criteria.

After each of these obstacles, you either received the next invitation or you got a letter of regret.

At the top of Snobdom were the Pi Sigs, the exclusive domain of the stars. Naturally, this was the sorority to which I aspired. Choosing to rush Pi Sig was the ultimate chutzpah: we lived closer to Broadway than Lake Shore Drive, I didn't own a single Pringle cashmere sweater, and my nostrils had never seen a scalpel. And yet, who knows why, I made it through the three teas and attained nirvana.

It's hard to believe the extreme sophistication of Chicago's high school students at that time. For example, these high school sororities and fraternities hosted citywide dances that featured nationally known big bands, such as Tommy and Jimmy Dorsey and Artie Shaw. The dances were financed by selling hundreds of tickets to high school students all over the city, and they took place in the glamorous ballrooms of Chicago's elegant hotels.

As a girl, if you were invited to attend one of these affairs, you received a cleverly designed "bid," a token of the evening, in which you could note who asked you to dance and anything else you wanted to remember about the evening. As you accumulated these bids, it was customary to drape them in long streams down your bedroom walls, like trophies, which indeed they were.

A boy's evidence of social achievement was different. Membership in a popular fraternity helped, but it was far more important to be on one of the school's athletic teams. If neither of these were possible, you still could distinguish yourself by being a very good dancer—I mean a really good dancer. Think John Travolta in *Saturday Night Fever*. This was the era of swing dancing, requiring smooth moves, a bit of athleticism, and more than a dash of showmanship.

As a girl, if you were asked to dance with one of these stars and you looked good on the dance floor, your dance card was full. This skill was considered so significant, our school provided continuous music on the stage of our auditorium during lunch periods. This gave us a chance to bolt down lunch in fifteen minutes and spend the rest of the hour practicing and displaying our moves.

In addition to dances, our sororities and fraternities held frequent socials. These were small evenings, just for members and their dates. The highlight of these socials was an original skit, usually based on a current theme. The Pi Sigs were known for these entertainments. As a pledge, I was expected to come up with many of them. Serendipitously, this turned out to be the ideal breeding ground for my larval stage of skit writing, which I expanded into more immoderate efforts in college, and, finally, into elaborate fund-raising efforts for the sisterhood of Temple Emanuel, in Davenport, Iowa, after I was married.

In high school, I rarely performed in the shows I wrote. Despite the ease with which members of my family could burst into song—a cappella, at the drop of a suggestion—and my own earlier triumph as the radiant mother of Jesus, throughout my adolescence, I remained extremely self-conscious. I harbored the hope that I would undergo a magical transformation and turn into a butterfly like Hilda Henke, a classmate with long blonde hair and the voice of an angel. That didn't happen.

When you were a junior at Senn, you could declare a major if you had a special interest in something. In yet another remarkable display of chutzpah, given my practically pathological shyness, in my junior year I elected to become a "Player."

Players were budding thespians who put on our school plays. Our drama teacher, Miss Skillen, once an actress somewhere, had an amazing talent: she could silence a room of chattering teenagers with one devastating stare. When she turned her attention toward me, my blood turned to ice water and goose bumps erupted wherever they could find some skin. Despite all this, and the lump in my throat that threatened to block my airways, I forced myself to try out for parts, which I occasionally—miraculously—received.

Such was the ability of the aptly named Miss Skillen, she managed to knead me into a passable Titania, queen of the fairies in Shakespeare's *Midsummer Night's Dream*. (I wasn't that good, but I got a lot fewer catcalls than the guy who played Oberon, the king of the fairies.) By my senior year, Miss Skillen leavened me to stardom as Lady Precious Stream in the play of the same name. I had improved by then, but it's possible that I got this part because the costume was small, and I was easily orientalized with a stroke of an eyebrow pencil.

During the last two years of high school, couples began to pair off and go steady. I tried this once or twice briefly, but I liked dating many boys, especially the good dancers. And I preferred non-threatening relationships that wouldn't "get out of hand," which was, in these days, "out of the question." Of course, a steady stream of intriguing rumors circulated through the school from time to time, and occasionally someone dropped out of school and disappeared.

Although being a virgin when you were married was

extremely important if you were a girl, you hoped your future husband wouldn't be, because it was his job to guide you through the churning rapids of whitewater sex. I went off to college unsullied; it wasn't even close.

Life in the 'Burbs, Oak Park, Illinois

"To those of you who received honors, awards and distinctions, I say well done. And to the C students, I say you, too, may one day be president of the United States."
—George W. Bush

Just a few months before my graduation from high school, Dad upstaged me by announcing a graduation of his own: he was leaving Morris Fisheries, taking on a partner, and going into business for himself. That was the good news. The bad news was, we were moving again. This time to Oak Park, a suburb west (not north) of Chicago, just three months before my graduation. My parents seemed to stay up nights thinking up ways to ruin my life.

For me to express this as bad news is an uncharacteristic understatement. It would not be hyperbole to say that I regarded this to be a major catastrophe, practically worthy of suicide. Here I was, at the top of my game at Senn, about to graduate with all my friends, dating Robin Hood (the star of our latest school production, *Robin Hood and His Merry Men*), and my unfeeling parents were banishing me to the boondocks.

To protest this heinous act, I pulled out all the stoppers: I cried, I threatened, I stopped speaking to everyone (which was probably a relief to them). Before I could gather up the courage to hurl myself off the rocks in Belmont Harbor, two members of Senn's faculty who happened to live in Oak Park stepped forward and offered to drive me to and from school every day until graduation.

Once I realized that Armageddon would not be happening, I accepted our move to the 'burbs with as much good grace as I could muster, which wasn't much. It helped when I discovered that our new house was glamorous and huge. We seemed to have ascended to another socioeconomic level—maybe to a whole new realm.

There were five of us when we moved in, but we soon became six, because my brother, Paul Richard, was born during this, our brief mansion period. Paul was named for Dad's new partner, Paul S., who turned out to be a cross between Benedict Arnold and Carl Icahn, but the family never called my brother Paul Richard, or even Richard, anyway. He became Rick almost immediately, partially because of the treachery, but also to complete our parents' rhyming roll call: Donnie, Ronny, Vicki, and now Ricky. Since Mother could never came up with the name of the child she wanted on the first try, we were doomed to hear that roll call ad nauseam through our lives as she proceeded down the list until she reached the one she wanted.

The new house was opulent. It not only accommodated all of us lavishly, it could have handled another couplet had my parents been so inclined. Vicki and Rick had separate bedrooms upstairs, near Mother and Dad's suite, and there was an a sitting room and several baths on that level. Downstairs, in addition to Ron's room, my room, and our shared bath, there was a formal living room, a formal dining room, the kitchen, a breakfast room, and the "maid's quarters," consisting of a small bedroom and bath. While we lived in the house, the title of "maid" was bestowed on a steady stream of candidates who rarely seemed to last more than one paycheck.

Just inside the front door, there was a reception room, with a curved staircase Norma Desmond would have envied. She could have descended majestically from her palatial bedroom suite on the second floor—my parents' accommodations, complete with a raised blue marble bathtub—pausing dramatically at the threshold of the sitting room at the top of the stairs before floating gracefully down to the landing. Hesitating there for pictures, she would be framed to great advantage by a two-story window opulently draped in folds of maroon velvet. This was early Hollywood at its best—way beyond anything my mother could have dreamed up in any of her decorating periods. And it all came with the house.

Like Virginia Woolf, I had longed for a room of my own during our Belmont days, and now I had one. It was next to the bathroom with a sunken tub, which I shared only with Ron, whose bedroom was next to mine. We had our own wing down the hall from the entrance hall and the living room. The distinguishing feature of the living room was the recessed cove lighting, designed to cast a soft, pink glow over the entire room and its occupants. It came furnished with assorted couches and chairs, all upholstered in the same color as the velvet drapery in the entrance hall.

Our family's only addition to the living room was a brand new rear-projection television set, a housewarming gift from friends. Television was still a new phenomenon then, and rear-projection sets were rare because they were more expensive. Their benefit was a bigger screen, but this was a questionable advantage, as there was nothing to view back then but test signals, *Howdy Doody*, and *The Gabby Hayes Show.*

Since the whole house came furnished, Mother's modern blonde furniture from Belmont Avenue was all sold, even the glass-topped table with its feather legs, which I never saw again. There were already two focal points in the basement: a white baby grand piano, somewhat out of tune but with its ivory keys still intact, and a built-in bar with a sink, a big mirror, and glass shelves— upon which we placed our pitiful collection of whiskey bottles and unmatched glasses.

My parents were not drinkers, although Mom told me she once drank three martinis, skipped dinner, went directly to a slice of apple pie à la mode, and didn't throw up. My sibs don't believe this story. The mother they knew reached an altered state of happy giggling after two sips of a margarita. Of course, they didn't know her in her blonde bombshell glory days.

We lived in the Oak Park house for several weeks before we discovered the secret room in the basement, discretely placed between the recreation room and the laundry room, which you couldn't see from the hall. After we found it, the secret room became the subject of many lively family discussions. What sinister function took place in this room?

The former owners were already the source of much

speculation. We knew he was a doctor of some kind, but none of us had ever seen him. Then, shortly after we moved in, we noticed that his wife drove up along side of the house every day and parked her car by the garage, where she remained for hours. Mother, an avid reader of detective stories, was convinced the secret room had been the scene of the doctor's illicit operations—either abortions or drugs.

His wife's strange behavior was harder to explain, but there was enough theater in the gauzy hangings, the velvet draperies, and the pink lighting of the house to support any drama my mother might have imagined. I think she pulled the story together by concluding that the wife was a former actress who had become a drug addict due to her husband's access to drugs. Lacking my mother's imagination, Dad's only contribution to the family's speculation was to point out that the room would have been a good place to keep a double set of books.

Three months after our move to Oak Park, I graduated from Senn and left this luxury to enter the University of Iowa and the world of army surplus. It was the fall of 1949. My new home on the Iowa City campus was in one of the Quonset huts hastily erected on the banks of the Iowa River to house the rising tide of incoming students, which now included hundreds of returning servicemen.

We could not have guessed that my parents were about to leave this splendor and embark on their own life-changing journey. During my freshman year, my father's partner executed a successful *coup d'état* by persuading a key employee to throw his shares to him, which gave Dad's partner more than fifty percent of the business. My father was immediately squeezed out. He was stunned. If there had been any clues, he missed them. He was an uncomplicated man, not intuitive and not sensitized to nuances or subtleties.

It was a bitter time for us. I was home for a school break when Dad told me about it. He took me upstairs to one of the outside decks so we could be alone. I didn't understand the details he was explaining at first, but when he said he couldn't afford to send me back to Iowa for another year, I was devastated. So was he. He looked so vulnerable and exposed, I had to look away; it felt as if I had witnessed a familiar actor without his stage makeup.

Characteristically, it didn't take him long to pull himself together and move on. Maybe he had experienced enough setbacks in his life to know he would recover from this one, but I'm not sure my mother ever got over this blow. It wasn't the loss of the house or the prestige. This was a bigger loss—I think she stopped believing in my father.

They sold the house and moved to New Orleans. He was a shrimp broker, so it seemed logical to Dad to move closer to the source of the product he sold. Mother may have stopped believing in him, but despite this horrendous experience, he still believed in himself. And he wasn't afraid to take on another partner. This time he made an excellent choice: Ted Shepard was an established Louisianan who knew the shrimp business as well as Dad did. Besides, as a minor figure in local politics, he also understood the internal workings of the territory. This being New Orleans, the territory was colorfully delineated as Orleans, Jefferson, Plaquemine, St. Bernard, and St. Tammany Parishes.

If you could measure the betrayal on a Richter scale, its force was extensive enough to change the course of our lives dramatically. New Orleans turned out to be good for Dad but bad for Mother. He had the resiliency to recover, but Mother's cumulative exposure to the ups and downs of their financial life left her with a fragile sense of security. She lost her snap. The close friendships she left behind in Sioux City and Chicago were never replaced in New Orleans.

For my sibs, the move meant immediate educational and social challenges akin to living in a foreign country. For me, it was an abrupt end to my incubation before I was ready to leave the protective womb of college life; it left me yearning for that feeling of unlimited possibilities I had experienced in Iowa City. The yearning lasted for long time, but more about this later.

In the end, it all worked out. Dad and his partner, Ted, were a good team, and their business prospered. They remained partners and good friends until Dad retired. As for the rest of us, we all learned to make lemonade, each in our own flavor.

Iowa City and My Brief Encounter with Academic Life

"If you don't know where you are going,
any road will get you there."
—Lewis Carroll

Blissfully unaware that my gestation was to end prematurely, due to the cruel forceps of parental misfortune—to extend my metaphor way beyond the limits of good taste, I arrived in Iowa City untethered and ready for Life (the capital is not a mistake). My view was that everything up to now was preparation. I was about to experience the real thing.

I traveled to the university by train with three other Chicago girls. Although we had gone to different high schools and didn't know each other, we were all from Chicago's North Side, and we were all Jewish. Sharing those two factors was a shortcut to complete cultural understanding. It even had binding properties, like the tzimmes I mentioned earlier. During those few hours on the train together, we congealed into the "Chicago Four," our collective identity at school that year.

The bucolic campus that sprawled along both sides

of the Iowa River and overflowed up the surrounding hills captivated us immediately. Of course, there were those utilitarian Quonset huts—hickeys on the otherwise perfect cheeks of the campus—where, as freshmen, we would be living. Since we were all assigned to the same one, the one closest to the Student Union and to the riverbank, we remained enraptured—until we opened the door and walked in.

Quonset huts probably come in many shapes and sizes; some might even be charming, with fireplaces, chintz, and window seats. But ours was one large rectangle lined with bunk beds and dressers on both sides of the two long walls. One short wall had a rod with a plastic curtain extending from one end to the other, unsuccessfully cordoning off a disaster area that included clothes, baggage, laundry bags, and some things that defied description. On the other short wall was the door leading to the Quadrangle, the series of matched brick buildings where most of our classes were held.

Adjacent to the main room of the Quonset hut was a small, communal bathroom with all the essentials and none of the luxuries, like privacy. Twelve of us were going to share these accommodations, we learned; it was a full house. By the time we got there, our eight roommates had taken possession of the best bunks. The ones that were left were farthest from the bathroom and closest to the outside door. This meant we could look forward to standing in a line to use the bathroom and being disturbed by our roommates' comings and goings when we were trying to study or sleep.

Of the twelve of us, we four were the only ones from a big city. Our roommates were from places like

Bartlesville, Oklahoma; Big Springs, Nebraska; and Pine Bluff, Arkansas. The only thing we seemed to have in common was the need to use the bathroom at the same time.

I had never been to camp, so a bunk with a lumpy mattress near a drafty door was a little more primitive than my picture of dormitory life. I was imagining a page out of *Seventeen* magazine. This was more like a page from *Field and Stream*. Calling on my inherited resources, I began my own knipple. From my small weekly stipend from Dad (always enclosed in a cheery letter written in green ink), I eventually saved enough for a bulletin board and a colorful orange bedspread imprinted with cactus plants, which I thought added a warm touch of Southwestern life to a chilly Iowa winter.

Even with the returning servicemen, the entire freshman class at Iowa was about the same size as my graduating high school class. This was comforting. After all, I had managed to survive the perils of Senn High School's caste system, the hazards of the sorority, and Miss Skillen's evil eye. Trudging across the Quadrangle with everyone else, the prevailing ambience appeared to be more egalitarian. If there were "stars" here, they were hard to spot in the undistinguished mass of students in ordinary clothes trudging across the Quadrangle, hustling to classes, or hanging out on blankets along the riverbank.

Entering freshmen were required to take a battery of tests. I could have predicted my results: I was exempt from English, but I had to take math skills. My exemption meant I could choose two electives. This was more freedom than I had known in any school, and maybe in life. I chose philosophy and modern literature.

Having been given such autonomy, I began to see the university as a road to a bigger life. Before long, however, I realized that sovereignty had a dark side: nobody would remind me that there was a test on Friday, and nobody would do my laundry. No one would even provide me with soap powder for the washing machine or the change for the dryer. Independence was not quite the rosy picture I had imagined; in fact, being in charge of myself was a heavy-duty responsibility.

On the other hand, I loved my classes—particularly my electives, and especially philosophy. In philosophy, we grappled with ethics, logic, and values—all the significant questions of life. It was exciting and challenging. Unlike most of my classes at Senn, these were subjects worth studying.

From being an indifferent student in high school (where I had been busy learning other things) I easily made the dean's list. Not only was the road bigger, I was bigger. I felt I was discovering new aspects of myself that had been waiting to be discovered. I wouldn't compare it with Michelangelo when he carved David; it was more like Geppetto whittling Pinocchio.

Accompanying my academic rush was an intoxicating social rush. The Chicago Four seemed to be invited to every event taking place on campus, particularly the Jewish ones. Yet, despite all this excitement and the lure of our escalating personal potential, within a month all four of us were in exclusive relationships. What was our hurry? Did we unconsciously consider marriage to be the real mission of a higher education? Was our book of future possibilities totally blank after the marriage page?

It seems strange now—with women firmly entrenched in every profession—but my generation had very few models of independent women with careers outside the home and even fewer models within our own families. Of course, there were the girls who were motivated to work for economic reasons; the ones who had grown up longing for a specific career, often in the helping professions, nursing or teaching; and the smaller select group, recognized to have special talents or abilities.

The option of an independent life didn't occur to the rest of us. In my case, despite the thrill of all those possibilities I was sensing, just a few months into my freshman year—way before I knew I would not be going back in school in the fall—I fell madly in love, and I was married a year later.

There is a Jewish word *bashert*. The word suggests our fate is preordained. We wrestled with this interesting question in my philosophy class. Do we exercise free will, or are we just pawns in a rigged chess game? We never concluded anything on a global scale. On a personal level—through retrospective rumination, which I happen to be really good at—I have come to believe that some things, if not truly preordained, may be inevitable.

For instance, I met Larry, my future husband, a few weeks into my freshman year. Through hindsight (my anatomically superior kind by far), I have come to realize that the stage for our relationship was set much earlier.

I first met him at his fraternity's dance. I had been fixed up with one of his fraternity brothers, a very nice football player, but we quickly ran out of things to talk about. It was going to be a long evening. Then I noticed Larry, and he noticed me. We danced once and chatted briefly, but that was it.

The following week I saw him at a Hillel mixer. Neither of us had ever attended anything there, but since its mission is to connect Jewish students and perpetuate Jewish life, I would have to say it was right on the money with us. Although it was crowded, I saw him immediately. There was just something arresting about him: flashing white teeth, erect carriage, and that riveting, inscrutable way he looked at me. I wasn't surprised to see him work his way over to where I was standing and begin a conversation.

Shazam! That's all it took. After that, we were together nearly every afternoon and every night, studying in the library, going to dinner, or just talking and watching the ducks in a nearby city park. Despite the automobile shortage after the war, Larry had a new car, a black Chevrolet coupe, capable of zipping up the snowy hills around the campus. (Zippy though it was, we managed to get stuck a few embarrassing times and had to be towed out of some fairly inaccessible places.)

Larry—we called him Sonny then—was elegant and worldly. In addition to these significant qualifications for husbandhood, he wore cashmere sweaters, had impeccable manners, ordered expertly from a menu, and always remembered to pull out my chair at dinner. I wish I could present myself as a deeper person, one with better values, but I don't think you're supposed to lie about yourself in your memoir. May I point out in my defense, I was then a shallow seventeen-year-old who had only recently graduated from her dancing stage into her full-bloom "upward mobility" stage?

Actually, that wasn't all I admired about Larry. He was a grown-up; he was grounded and sensible. Maybe that was because his future was clear. He knew he would live in Davenport, a town only sixty miles from Iowa City, and go into the family jewelry business. I, of course, had no plans at all yet. I was still mulling over possibilities.

Larry also had a more advanced social sense then I did. I was happy with my current friends, but he thought I should join the Jewish sorority and expand my social horizons. (He was going to love my mother.) I took his advice. After what I had been through with the Pi Sigs, joining this sorority was painless. And joining it was a good idea. As a pledge, I was back to writing skits and producing shows, which reinforced the skills I was to use over and over again throughout my life.

It was easy for us to imagine spending our lives together. We glided into our relationship as effortlessly as the nearby ducks floated on their pond. We seemed to be a perfect match. In his senior year, Larry was elected president of his fraternity, and I was voted the fraternity's sweetheart. We met each other's parents and talked about getting married someday. I thought I was going to take more philosophy classes and declare a major in contemporary literature, but as the Jewish proverb so aptly goes, "Man plans and God laughs." (It's better in Yiddish because it rhymes: *Mentsch Tracht und Gott Lacht.*)

But the world was changing. Not only would I have to leave school and find a job somewhere, the Korean War erupted. It was 1950. The army began to draft unmarried men Larry's age. Since we planned to marry eventually anyway, his parents suggested that we think about a Thanksgiving wedding. Shortly after we began to plan our wedding, we learned that Larry had been rejected from the army because of his allergies.

We had a Thanksgiving wedding as planned. I was nineteen and he was twenty. I was okay, but he required a letter of permission from his parents.

So was it bashert? I don't know. But even if it wasn't truly preordained, sixty years later and divorced for thirty, I still can see how perfectly we fit together at the time.

Once, though, before Larry and I made the commitment to date only each other, I had a couple of dates with a senior in medical school. He was interesting, and he was a great kisser. I found myself swept along in the moment. He seemed to know more about my body than I did.

If I hadn't been so intent on saving myself for marriage, I might have realized he would have been a wise and skillful guide to lead me through the churning rapids of whitewater sex.

He clearly thought so, too.

One night at a fraternity party, when the three of us were standing together, he confronted Larry. He had been drinking. He proposed that since he was about to graduate and Larry had another semester, Larry should shove off and find someone else.

There was a noisy altercation and a Coke bottle was smashed. When I looked down, I realized my ankle had been cut by a piece of glass and was bleeding. The thrill of being fought over was gone. It was Larry who took me to the hospital and stayed with me while I was stitched up. This ended any lingering thoughts I might have had about that tour guide. And in case I ever forget, I still have a little scar on my left ankle.

Fate is a funny thing. Whether or not it's bashert.

Married Life, from Iowa City to Davenport

"In olden times, sacrifices were made at the altar, a practice that still continues."
—Helen Rowland

After our November wedding, we came home to a small basement apartment Larry felt lucky to find in view of the severe housing problem in Iowa City. We lived there until he graduated in February. It was a long three months—long enough for the apartment to etch itself indelibly into my mind.

Let's just say you wouldn't find our apartment pictured in any magazine with which you may be familiar, not even as a "before" in a magazine like *Popular Mechanics*. Finding our apartment at all was a challenge for the uninitiated. You had to walk around to the back door of the house, maneuver a flight of narrow wooden stairs to the basement, and then grope through the landlady's ever-present washing to reach our unpainted, unvarnished, untreated plywood door.

Once in the living room, a lumpy Salvation Army couch and a chair of the same provenance greeted you. The only light in the room was provided by the floor lamp next to the space heater. There was no ignoring the heater's squat knobby presence because it was the apartment's only source of heat and it was a damp, snowy November.

From the living room, you entered the kitchen with its small, wooden table and two dissimilar chairs, one plastic and chrome, the other wooden with a crack down the center of the seat. Then you could turn right and enter our bedroom or go straight ahead into the bathroom.

The bathroom possessed the apartment's only architectural frill, a big shower with a built-in bench. The bench was big enough for two occupants. This confused us. Were we meant to sit on the bench while we washed our feet? Wash each other's feet? Something else? The only thing missing in our bathroom was a sink. Since the sink could have been installed in about the same amount of space as the bench, we concluded it was an esthetic decision on the part of the builder.

Nothing about the bedroom was memorable, except possibly the mattress on the double bed, which undulated like a Grant Wood landscape. Not even the heavy corduroy monogrammed bedspread—a touch of class provided by Larry's parents, Maymie and Sam—could disguise its hills and valleys.

The bedspread wasn't our only nod to refinement. I brought a trousseau with me. Every bride came with one back then, but mine was heavy on organza bridge sets and cocktail napkins. It didn't include anything useful, like kitchen towels. All of this was insignificant to me. I looked at this marriage as my new major, and I was programmed to give it my best shot. (I had the will, if not the talent, of an early Martha Stewart.)

I wasn't blind to the limitations of our apartment, but

I wasn't prepared for its effect on our first guests, Maymie and Sam. Maymie managed to glue on a permanent smile, but Sam took one look around and broke into noisy tears, honking into his handkerchief and wiping his eyes.

Like the Greeks, Maymie and Sam always came bearing gifts. In addition to giving us the monogrammed bedspread, this time they brought us a small chicken they called a "capon." We thanked them warmly. I was too embarrassed to admit I didn't know what it was or what to do with it. Fortunately, we had a dictionary and a copy of *The Settlement Cookbook*, the comprehensive bible given to every Jewish bride in those days—it wouldn't have been Julia Child's pick, but it was a lot more useful than a trousseau of elegant luncheon cloths.

From the dictionary, I learned that a capon was a castrated young male, a procedure that apparently produced a juicier, meatier bird. Always on the side of the underdog, in this case on the side of an underchicken, I personally thought this was very drastic procedure just to produce a slightly better dinner. I moved quickly to *The Settlement Cookbook,* where I learned that the cook should begin by washing the bird and plucking any stray feathers.

Intimidated but determined, I placed the unfortunate bird in the kitchen sink—our only sink—and began to follow the book's directions. First I washed it carefully with bar soap and water. Then I plucked out anything suspicious with my tweezers. What I did after that is a blur, except that I do remember stuffing it with Rice-A-Roni. This was the beginning of many culinary adventures I would set before Larry.

Since he was still going to school and I wasn't attending

classes, I felt it was my job to get up first and light the pilot on the space heater. It had two settings, "off and cold" and "on and hot," so this was not a time-consuming procedure. What was time-consuming was what came next. According to the women's magazines I was reading now, it was important, and apparently a lot harder, to keep the flame going in your husband. (His knobs were less visible.) Dutifully, I took their advice and appeared each morning fully dressed, complete with makeup. I did this surreptitiously to give the impression that I looked this good without any help.

After adorning me, I adorned breakfast. Grapefruit had to be sectioned and broiled. The cherry was optional. If we were having eggs, it had to be an omelet—cheese, mushroom, or Denver. A cold bowl of cereal wasn't even an option. I was finding married life exhausting.

Fortunately or unfortunately, depending on how you looked at it, I wasn't the only one intent on introducing style and graciousness into our subterranean life. In addition to attending classes, Larry now became the self-appointed czar of our social life. A latent "let's-give-a-party" gene suddenly emerged, no doubt inherited from his accomplished mother, who could make chopped liver, beef tenderloin, and a schaum torte without opening a book.

I think we entertained nearly every weekend we lived in Iowa City. We gave dinner parties, cocktail parties, coffee klatches, and an occasional Sunday brunch. What I lacked in skill I made up for in imagination, but no triumphs come to mind. I do remember a few misdemeanors, like the time I basted a steak with bourbon because we didn't have any sherry and the time I got caught pouring small amounts of scotch from various bottles into one nicely full bottle. This seemed to be a logical, efficient way to consolidate our supply, but Larry regarded my act as a felony just short of treason.

After graduation, we followed our script. We moved to Davenport, and Larry went to work in the family store. Until we found a place of our own, we were invited to move into a spare bedroom in Maymie and Sam's large and gracious home (later bought by Johnny Lujack, quarterback for the Chicago Bears and a Heisman Trophy winner). Our accommodations could hardly be described as "spare." We were given Larry's married sister Marilyn's former bedroom, glamorously appointed with white loopy carpeting, mirrored tables, an upholstered headboard, a dressing alcove, and a large private bathroom.

This move was always going to be temporary, but it was more temporary than we planned. As big as the house was, we were never alone, and no house is big enough for two housekeepers, even if one is just an apprentice. Having no furniture to go with our nonexistent linen collection (my trousseau didn't include sheets either), we rented a furnished efficiency apartment downtown in the Blackhawk Hotel. The good thing was, this apartment had a sink in the bathroom and another one in the kitchen. The bad thing was, neither room was big enough for both of us to occupy at the same time.

The living room, however, was large and gracious—perfect for entertaining. We might not have our own furniture, but we had plenty of appointments, all of which we received as wedding presents. Our inventory included silver trays, bone china, sterling silver, and every appliance made by Sunbeam, the line of small appliances carried in the family jewelry store. Since we had no books, we displayed these gifts prominently on the built-in bookshelves above the twin couches that served as our beds at night. There was also a small alcove off the living room that served as a dinette, which we discovered could seat up to six friendly guests.

Now that Larry was working, entertaining fell to me. There was a slight complication to having dinner parties here. Although we could set a splendid table using our own appointments and our living room was large enough to accommodate twelve people graciously, electrical outlets were scarce. There was one in the kitchen and one meant for shaving in the bathroom light fixture. This led to a snarl of extension cords, frequent overloads, and blown fuses. We learned to live with deep fryers and bun warmers in the bathroom and cords dangling from the light fixture down the mirror to the commode, but it was hard to pull off an elegant dinner party with these off-stage dramas occurring at the worst possible times.

In addition to entertaining, it now became my job to manage our finances. I knew nothing about budgets or money management. Why would I? I never had any money of my own. Undaunted, if this was going to be my job, I was prepared to meet the challenge the way I met every challenge. I went to the library and researched the subject.

I found a book on budgeting that was big on illustrations and bulleted copy. It promised to provide a simple, foolproof method for beginners. I particularly liked the chapter that suggested you organize your budget into household categories. I counted the categories of our life and purchased the proper expandable file from the office supply store. It even came with labels. I removed the Gideon Bible from the drawer in the living room desk and dedicated that space to budgeting. I was ready for Larry to bring home his first paycheck. As it turned out, it would have been more useful to read the Bible.

The plan was simple enough: Larry would cash his check, and I would put a preordained amount into each of the labeled compartments. The benefit of this plan, the book said, was that it would teach us to live within our means. The plan was doomed from the start. Our Rent category was much higher than the allotted and recommended one-fourth of Larry's paycheck, and it didn't help that every month we spent twice as much on Entertainment as we did on Food.

I soon discovered that the expandable file was missing some important compartments. Which compartment was supposed to cover gifts? What about books and magazines? Car repairs? Our Miscellaneous file began to swell dangerously, and Savings shrank to a sliver. I didn't learn how to live within our means with that system. I learned how to rob Peter to pay Paul, and I could have learned that from the Gideon Bible.

It was clear we had to move to a cheaper apartment as soon as we could afford furniture. But the categories of Furniture and What We Could Afford fell under Maymie's jurisdiction. Accompanied by a family friend who owned a furniture store and could get us into the Merchandise Mart in Chicago, we bought two rooms of French Provincial furniture wholesale and moved into an upstairs apartment of a duplex in an old, undistinguished neighborhood, hoping to save enough money to buy a house someday.

It was here, in this humble upstairs apartment on West 15th Street, decorated with upscale French furniture and burnt-orange burlap curtains—an idea I saw in *House Beautiful,* my new favorite magazine—that I once served undercooked chicken to a houseful of guests. They later became our lifelong friends and never let me forget it. It was also here that our first child was born, then Julie Beth, now known as Ashely, and where, eighteen months later, our second one showed up, Jonathan David.

Although I never mastered Budgeting 101 and our savings never grew much, we had run out of space. With our next move, my job description would grow to include all the tasks associated with building a house. These included dealing with contractors, negotiating additional electrical outlets without paying extra for them, and learning to live with mistakes that couldn't be changed. The last was the hardest—and it still is. Eventually the house was finished, and we moved in. We took the French Provincial furniture, but we left the expandable file and the burnt-orange burlap curtains behind.

Building Dreams, Part 1: The House on Kohler Drive

"People are living longer, a phenomenon made necessary by the 30-year mortgage."
—Doug Larson

Our third and last baby, Jane Martha, was born a few weeks after we moved into our first house. Since I labored over every detail of that house, I felt I had given birth twice. Jane turned out well, but the house fell short of my attempt to elevate an off-the-rack model into one-of-a-kind couture.

It was now 1956, the era of the split-level house. Our street could be described as an epidemic of split-levels with infections of various colors. Two things distinguished our house from the others: We had a pot of red geraniums at the front door, which looked just as good there as it did on the cover of *House Beautiful* where I had seen it. And our living room windows, designed to open horizontally, had been installed upside down, a distinction that only surfaced after our first drenching rain.

The thing about split-level houses, which is not apparent from the blueprints, is that you never seem to be on the right level for anything you need or want to do. For example, our entrance hall was on the same level as the garage, powder room, and laundry room. You could go up a few steps to the living room, dining room, and kitchen, from which you could climb more steps to the bedrooms and baths. Or you could forget the whole thing, descend to our exposed basement, and make yourself a drink.

For the meticulous or for those suffering from OCD, which might be the same thing, life in a split-level house could easily become a cardiovascular opportunity. I learned to circumvent this problem by piling things on steps until some compelling reason required me to ascend or descend farther.

Although I didn't quite succeed in upgrading our house to the level of couture, I did come up with a few unusual touches. From a decorator, I learned that the first wall you see when you walk into a house should be considered the "accent" wall. That wall, she explained, should establish the tone for the entire house. After thinking obsessively about this, I installed some discontinued white brick wallpaper on our accent wall in the entrance hall. To add to the ambience, I glued a brass clock directly in the middle of the wall. It looked great, until the day a cold-air register appeared directly above it. It was only place it could go, our builder explained, a small detail he had failed to mention in advance.

This failure fueled my resolve to create an unobstructed accent wall in the living room. The first visible wall there happened to extend from the living room through the dining room—the entire width of the house. I decided to wallpaper this expanse in a lovely neutral-colored burlap. I was still hooked on burlap, which I read was the perfect background for the art collection I was sure we would accrue through the years.

Perhaps I was thinking about the Annenbergs, because when we moved in, our art collection was limited to one canvas. I am sure the burlap *would* have been a great background for our art collection. Except that we were slow in collecting, and our cat, Chou Chou, was quick to discover that burlap made a great scratching post. Then she realized it also provided the traction she needed to climb the wall. It became her favorite game to hang from the top like a suicide, meowing for help.

I had better results applying my creativity to the transformation of our exposed basement. Like a chef creating a signature dish, I spent weeks planning, rejecting, adding another ingredient, until I was satisfied that everything was right. It was. This time there were no hitches. The basement was now a recreation room, with an adjoining office/library. Only a small area in the back was devoted to the equipment you usually find filling up a basement, like the furnace.

Accomplishing this required disguising pipes and knobs and fuse boxes. It had demanded every scintilla of problem-solving skills I could scrape together. When everything was installed, every protuberance concealed, and my last to-do list was crumbled and thrown away, I went into labor with Jane. Our babies were all very thoughtful about their births. They chose to be born after my kitchen cabinets were straightened and when Larry's store was closed. As they grew up, they became less considerate, but I digress.

When you had a baby in those days, you stayed in the hospital for a week. Then, if you could afford it, a practical nurse came home with you for a week. Jane was born in December during an extended major freeze, so characteristic of an Iowa winter. The night we came home from the hospital, as Mrs. Clevenger, our nurse, was preparing Jane's midnight feeding, I heard an ominous sound that could only mean trouble. It was coming from our newly finished basement, which I secretly considered to be my finest hour (Churchill had his, I had mine).

Racing to the disastrous sound, I was transfixed by the sight of ceiling plaster floating like icebergs on our handsome new black and white floor. Ankle-deep water covered everything. Not only had our tile floor disappeared, so had all the legs of our furniture, and water was still gushing from broken pipes near the ceiling, which, apparently, had not been protected sufficiently for this prolonged cold snap.

It took months to restore order. But such is the restorative power of the human soul, by spring we were busy landscaping. We planted a Moraine Locust tree in the front yard, a row of poplar trees along the back, and flowering bushes along the sides of the house. Under the dining room window, I planted a small rose garden. My domestic skills were about to expand to spraying and cultivating. My vocabulary would soon include "black spot," "mildew," and "brown canker."

We observed many lifecycle events in the years we lived in Kohler Drive. Our children grew to adolescence. Chou Chou was buried, and Pepper, a standard poodle, came to live with us. Pepper spent his entire life with us on leash—in and out of the house—because of his nasty predilection to bite our guests and most of us. We eventually gave up on him and took him to a nearby farm to live. We threw in the leash.

While we lived here, Maymie and Sam retired and moved to Florida. A few years later, Paul, Larry's brother and business partner, and his wife, Janet, moved there too. Larry became more and more absorbed in the store. Over time, his preoccupation grew and gave rise to something I used to call his "Sunday Night Noodie," a name I invented that somehow fit the silent withdrawal that hit him after dinner Sunday night and lasted until he left for work on Monday morning.

As for me, I took English classes at all the local colleges and then began to commute to Iowa City for one-to-one tutorials. Timidly, I began to write short pieces, which I sent to various publications. The mail delivery became the highlight of my day—particularly when I received an acceptance letter, but even on the days a rejection slip included a personal note.

When I had taken enough classes to fulfill the requirement for a major in English literature, I began to wonder what it was that I was missing. But I didn't spend much time thinking about it, because we decided to build a bigger house.

Building Dreams, Part 2: The House on Pineacre Avenue

"There must be more to life than having everything."
—Maurice Sendak

When we built the Pineacre house, I imagined we would live in it the rest of our lives. That was the dream I was building along with the house. The stars seemed to be properly aligned: our lot was directly across the street from the house where Larry's aunt and uncle, Edna and Ben, had lived for years. They were my favorite Siegels. We had spent many lovely evenings with them in their gracious home. I hoped we would be able to recreate that same cordiality and warmth in our own house across the street.

We positioned the house on the crest of the hill, on a corner where two sloping streets bisected each other. It was a charming traditional neighborhood with awnings, flowerbeds, two-car garages, weather vanes, and basketball hoops. From the beginning, the house was destined to be solely my project. I found the plan in a magazine and worked with an architect to modify it to fit our needs and for the shape of the lot. Larry was remodeling the store at the same time and was too preoccupied to take much interest. Looking back, this was a perfect metaphor for the two-track marriage ours had become.

The house was lovely when it was finished, an attractive blend of brick, shutters, and hand-split shakes. Euonymus vines climbed to the second story. In the back yard, above it all, towered a magnificent Colorado blue spruce that had stood guard over the land for over a hundred years.

Having explored the possibilities of our split-level house to ridiculous ends, this house was a time-honored, two-story floor plan: living room on one side of the entrance hall, dining room on the other. Strategically placed around this core were the kitchen, family room, and a formal living room—so formal that the only thing it was missing, my brothers commented, was a velvet rope to cordon off the riff-raff.

Upstairs, there were four bedrooms and two baths. This time, the basement was allowed to remain a real basement. Nothing was cleverly concealed down there. Standing prominently in the middle of the room was a large pool table with a supplemental ping-pong top, a present from my parents. A small room beyond served as an extra bedroom for spillover guests. Everything from Kohler Drive that didn't work upstairs landed there, including the piano (like my mother, I hoped to spark a musical fire in any of our children—and so far, my efforts had produced the same results.)

Thinking about the house, even after so many years, I can produce a scenario of a typical day there: Let's say it is mid-afternoon, after school. The screen door slams three times, announcing the presence of one after another of the children. There are kisses and cursory greetings all around. I am in the kitchen preparing dinner. As I watch, the round kitchen table in the center of the room becomes a repository for books, sacks of leftover lunches, sweaters, and gym suits brought home for me to wash. A pile of discarded shoes gathers under the table. Uninterrupted chatter accompanies this accumulation.

The refrigerator door opens and closes many more than three times. Children appear briefly in the doorway, still chattering, accompanied by peanut butter sandwiches, apples, and potato chips. Someone snaps on the television, and everyone disappears into the family room. A lively conversation ensues.

My daughter, complaining: "I want to watch Beaver!"

My son, assertively: "Well, I want to watch the Monkees!"

(*sounds of pummeling and protests*)

My other daughter, tearfully: "Mom, he never lets us watch our shows!"

In the kitchen, I open a can of something, maybe tomato sauce if we are having Italian. The cat (this one called Bogart), hearing the whirring sound of the electric can opener in the kitchen, enters the room majestically. He rubs against my leg, hoping that the sound of the can opener means liver or tuna will soon appear in his dish.

From the family room, the sound of the television set

being snapped on and off can be heard. Accompanying the sound is a chorus of accelerating voices, ranging from a guttural growl to a piercing screech.

> Both daughters, very exasperated: "Mom, aren't you going to do something about him? He's disgusting!"

The sound of an electric garage door rolling upward can be heard above the television, the can opener, the meowing cat, and the protests from the family room. The utility room door opens. My husband enters the kitchen. He offers a perfunctory kiss.

> My husband, annoyed: "I don't understand why you can't park your car closer to the wall. Every night I have to fight golf clubs, bicycles, and pop bottles."

He walks to the counter that serves as a bar and makes himself a martini, or perhaps it is a scotch. He looks at the mail as he stirs his drink.

> My husband, sighing: "Who is this invitation from? Oh, God. Do we have to go?"

I have moved into the dining room, where the walls and the carpet are a soft, serene wash of gold. At the moment, I am setting the table for five. In later years, I will set it for four, three, two—finally, just for me.

We didn't live in the Pineacre house for the rest of

our lives. On a recent visit to Davenport to see friends, I drove by the house. Not much was different outwardly. The shutters, the weathered, hand-split shakes, and the euonymus vines were all in place. So was the hundred-year-old spruce. Ben and Edna Siegel's house was still across the street. Yet, everything else had changed. We have all moved on to new homes and new lives.

This house, even more than the other outgrown houses I have written about here, will always remain with me. It was in this orderly, carefully orchestrated house of muted colors, wood paneling, wall-to-wall bookshelves, stereophonic music, laundry chutes that didn't end up in the right place, and built-in milk boxes we could squeeze through when keys were lost, that my life fell apart.

When other people talk about the Great Depression, they are referring to what happened in the world. When I talk about the Great Depression, I am talking about mine. The Pineacre house turned out to be a nightmare of *Mr. Blandings Builds His Dream House* proportions. Like the book and the movie, it was one crisis after another. What was estimated to take four or five months, symbolically took nine. Functioning as the general contractor, I was at the house every waking hour that the children were in school, dealing with unforeseen problems and surly subcontractors who either didn't like women or didn't like me. The hostility mounted into outright war.

I was exhausted. I felt totally alone—and being responsible for the biggest budget I would probably ever have didn't help. At least Mr. Blandings had Myrna Loy for support and Louise Beavers to cook dinner. I gave myself locker-room pep talks that Knute Rockne would envy. That worked for a while, and then nothing worked.

Dread became my constant companion. Cheekbones I hadn't seen for years surfaced. I couldn't sleep through the night, a captive audience of my ruminating thoughts. I watched the clock pass the hours until it was time to get up and do it all again. If my knowledge of human behavior back then had exceeded the "Dear Abby" column and Kinsey's books on sexual behavior, I might have recognized all these symptoms.

I entered therapy. I had to—it was either that or conduct the rest of my life from bed. I did not welcome the idea of lifting up the lid on what might turn out to be Pandora's box. What if Ms. Hyde was down there? What if I needed a lobotomy? What if this doctor—cheerfully recommended by our family physician, who had never been depressed in his life—wasn't any good?

Entering therapy was one of the best things I ever did, but I knew even then I might be committing myself to some irreversible action. My first therapeutic session was memorable. After a minute or two of small talk, the doctor asked me why I had come to see him. I began to tell him about the house, the workman, and the responsibility. Then I segued into Larry's growing preoccupation with the store. After a few more minutes of this, he stopped me.

"How are you feeling?" he asked.

For fifteen minutes I had been telling him. Wasn't he listening?

"Well," I started again. "I feel I'm going to live through this eventually..."

He stopped writing and looked up from his yellow pad. "I think so, too. But that's an opinion. I was asking about your feelings."

I pondered this for a while, puzzled by this distinction. I had plenty of opinions, but did I have any feelings?

"I don't know," I answered honestly. "I think I buried them. What can I do to find them?"

"Let's start with plus or minus," he suggested. "Right now, are you feeling plus or minus?"

And so it began, the process of exhuming my feelings. It took a few sessions for me to figure out that I did have feelings, and that I had been repressing for years. Especially my anger. Always an obedient child, seemingly born without a rebellion gene, I was raised to believe that expressing anger was not an appropriate reaction to anything less than rape or attempted murder.

After a few sessions, I began to get the hang of expressing my anger, and I was ready to practice on my husband who, incidentally, had no problem expressing *his* anger. His problem was expressing his feelings at the other end of the spectrum—love and intimacy. Together, we were a full-service emotional spectrum.

I chose to come out of the closet with something safe. A limited skirmish was what I had in mind. This may not be the exact dialogue, but it's pretty close:

> Me, one morning: "I am sick and tired of picking up your clothes. Collecting your underwear is not part of my job description, and I'm not going to do it anymore."
>
> Husband, confidently: "Oh, yes you will. You'll crack. You won't be able to stand it when cobwebs start forming on my socks."

Me: "I won't crack because whatever you leave on the floor is going out the window so I don't have to look at it."

Him: "Is this what you're learning in therapy? Can we take a vote? I definitely liked you better before."

But it was too late. I couldn't go back. The heartening thing about depression is, although it's painful and frightening, it can open new doors. Beyond the open doors is change and an opportunity to grow. Growth, however, can be risky. It can require you to leave what is familiar, what you may still love.

My husband and I had three lovely children together, we had a history, and we had a big, beautiful house. We had the trappings, but it was all a clever set. What was missing was a real relationship. Somehow the bond that accrues from love, intimacy, and trust never happened for us. After the kids all left, I think we both knew the play had come to an end.

Of course, this did not come as a total surprise. During our twenty-five years of marriage, we participated in several rounds of marriage counseling, alone and together. We even joined a "marriage encounter" class, after which half the class got divorced, including the leader. When that didn't work, we tried a trial separation, during which we "dated."

For our finale, we tried Masters and Johnson, the renowned clinic in St. Louis. We were such a big success there that we were dismissed early. Unfortunately, we had to leave our idyllic surroundings and go back to the real world.

It was very painful to leave Larry, because part of me still loved him—the "him" I married, who reappeared now and then on vacations. Then he stopped showing up, period. It was tough, but twenty-five years is a long enough to wait, even for Elijah.

It's difficult to encapsulate that tumultuous time. I offer this allegory instead.

Epitaph for a Marriage

On March 28, 1931, the stork delivered a small lump of protoplasm to a well-meaning couple who were hoping for just such a mass to mold, although a year or two later would have been better.

Said the woman, "Since it's a little girl, I will teach her how to be popular by being agreeable and non-assertive. I will see that she gets tap-dancing lessons and piano lessons. I will even teach her how roast a turkey under a foil tent, but I will never get around to teaching her how to make my sauce for the boiled shrimp."

And the man said, "I will teach her all the important things, like dogged determination even when she is drowning in a sea of defecation, because there might be a pony in there somewhere. I will teach her to press her lips together to control her temper, and by precept and example, I will demonstrate the importance of practicing her golf swing continuously on the slight chance that a permanent groove might happen."

As the little lump grew, she mastered all the lessons her parents provided. She became a courteous and thoughtful people-pleaser who always put others first. She was never angry, impatient, or disrespectful—outwardly. Even when the little girl became a teenager, she never rebelled. She did her homework (including the geometry), dated the right boys, and never cut classes (except once, to see Frank Sinatra in person). She remained pure as the driven snow until she got married, although she indulged in a little hanky-panky now and then.

When the little girl married at nineteen, she chose the perfect man and had three nearly perfect children. She volunteered in the community, voted in every election, visited the sick, and attended funerals—even the funerals of people she didn't like. But as the years passed, she grew more and more unhappy. She had no idea what could be wrong. She tried more vitamins, she exercised, she attended Friday night services, but her tears continued to fall.

She went to the library, as she always did when she was looking for answers, and read a lot of books. She read one called *The Lonely Crowd* by a sociologist named David Riesman. He said many apparently successful people were leading inner lives of desperation, especially the "other-directed" conformists. She read another book called *The Feminine Mystique,* by Betty Friedan, who seemed to be writing about the little girl.

After learning all this, she was still miserable, so she went to a psychiatrist. He said she was depressed because she was tired of playing Miss Good Housekeeping and she wanted to be a real girl now.

She tried to explain all this to her husband, hoping he might want to be real. But he said he liked his role, and he thought their marriage was fine the way it was. Although he said he understood what she was talking about, this was all he needed a marriage to be.

It was sad, but she had to accept the fact that the seductive web of exteriority they had spun together was a marriage to him. While for her, their marriage was like an elegant handkerchief in a breast pocket: all show and no blow.

The little girl had to go on without him because she had no choice. The growing process she had begun in therapy was like childbirth—it couldn't be stopped just because it hurt. She grew to recognize and express her feelings, although anger is still a problem on occasion. She also learned to consider her own needs and desires, but again, she is still working on this.

The moral to this allegory is, "It's better to be the rider than the horse, but if it's possible, try to be both."

And Dad, wherever you are, you were wrong. Sometimes, no matter how hard you try, there is no payoff. Even if you conquer your fears and become a pretty good Lady Precious Stream in the play of the same name, Hollywood doesn't write and doesn't call. And even if you are crowned the Sweetheart of Phi Epsilon Pi, the president may want you to remain an embryonic bud instead of a full-blown rose. Finally, even if your dinner parties are flawless, your marriage may fail. Especially if somewhere along the way, you change into a cantaloupe and he prefers to remain a watermelon.

As W.C. Fields put it: "If at first you don't succeed, try, try again. Then quit. There's no point in being a damn fool about it."

Way Down Yonder in New Orleans ...

"People in New Orleans never said
no, unless the question was,
'Are you ready to stop partying and go home?'"
—Drew Carey

While I was busy building nests and feathering them in Davenport, the rest of my family had abandoned the homogeneity of Oak Park, Illinois, for the diversity of the Crescent City. (To find New Orleans on a map, just look where the Mississippi bends like a duodenum to dump its fluids into the Gulf of Mexico.)

Even though my family didn't cross the plains of the Serengeti, I still think of their move as the Great Migration. In New Orleans, they found themselves enveloped in an exotic new culture where walking slowed to a saunter, frequent cokes were the drug of choice, and even the English language seemed to melt into a warm dialect.

"Nawlins," they learned, was a slurred reference to "New Orleans" and "wahta" was southern for "water." Instead of black-and-white names like "Dodge Street" or "Michigan Avenue," they were confronted by Technicolor names they couldn't pronounce. Streets called "Tchoupitoulas" and "Melpomene," for instance, sent them into fits of laughter.

From the white bread of Oak Park, my family now found itself submerged in a smorgasbord of French, Spanish, Indian, and African cultures. They were amazed and amused by it all, but it took a while for them to settle into their life there.

As was typical for my parents, "settling" was incremental. Tactical maneuvers took place over time. Their first apartment was an apartment on Florida Avenue (too far away and not Jewish enough). Next, they moved to a duplex on Nashville (not big enough and not convenient enough). Then came my mother's favorite, the high-rise on St. Charles called the Penthouse, with spectacular night views from the balcony. The spotlighted church steeples and elegant mansard roofs could have been a movie set in Paris starring Gene Kelly and Leslie Caron.

I remember this balcony vividly because it was there that Rick, newly graduated from John Hopkins and possessor of the only PhD in our family, turned to me and famously suggested that we "renegotiate our relationship" to something more collegial. I admit this suggestion is only famous to me and the multitudes to whom I have mentioned it over the years. I have tried that line myself in various relationships, but it has never worked for me. Maybe it requires a PhD.

My parents' final move was to the red brick duplex farther up St. Charles, near Carrollton. I'm not sure if this neighborhood is considered "Uptown" or the "Garden District," but it became home until everyone left New Orleans.

My parents sold all their furniture with the Oak Park

house. Nothing from Chicago or Oak Park made it down there. With their move to the St. Charles duplex, it was clear that Mother had entered her oriental period. The duplex was divided into two up-and-down residences, but her oriental period was reflected only downstairs, in the living and dining rooms. She furnished them in seriously unembellished furniture, which included an elegant, cream-colored silk Baker couch and two end tables (Jane and I each have one of these). Everything else was upholstered in black and brown, including two swiveling barrel chairs covered in a black and brown print reminiscent of Russian constructionist art (Vicki has these). On the walls were Picasso prints from his cubist period, framed in black (nobody took those).

Mother was not making a statement upstairs in the two baths and three bedrooms, unless it was "I'm not making a statement up here." The master bedroom was a lovely big room in the back of the house. It had its own bath and a small addition attached to it, which I immediately labeled "the nursery." Since there were no candidates available, it became Dad's workshop. A diligent student, born with a dominant perseverance gene, every night he practiced his putting and chip shots up there; it was a testament to his skill that the bedroom woodwork remained only slightly nicked. The boys, Ron and Rick, destined to be called "the boys" the rest of their lives unless they asked to renegotiate the label, shared the next room. It remained untouched, like Miss Haversham's chamber, even after they left home forever.

I slept there whenever I visited, unless of course the boys were visiting too. In that case, I slept in the front bedroom, which had no beds and no dresser—just one old bookcase and a recycled army cot Mother rented for these occasions. The cot came with a plastic-covered mattress. The plastic was never removed, no matter how long the rental period lasted. This may have been Mother's version of the Hippocratic oath, "First do no harm to the rented furniture," or it could have been a stray gene she picked up from Bobo.

Sleeping in the front bedroom required nerves of steel. The nocturnal cacophony of crinkling plastic, plus the *energico* of the clanging bell and clicking wheels of the St. Charles streetcar, which seemed to run all night just outside my bedroom, was reminiscent of the percussion section of my first-grade orchestra at Floyd School in Sioux City. There were three of us in that section, and we took turns playing the triangle, the bell, and a set of maracas, all of which we played with great gusto, extremely *forte* and *accelerando.*

Considering that none of us would characterize our parents by descriptors such as flexible, audacious, or venturesome—certainly not at this stage of their lives, anyway—it was amazing how quickly they adjusted to life in New Orleans. They had never bought cases of anything while I lived with them, but now a case of Coke was perennially stashed in the back hall. Not long after the Cokes, Hazel arrived, ostensibly as a cleaning lady, but soon to be as entrenched as the case of Coke.

The biggest surprise was the gustatory delight my entire family demonstrated toward the food of the region. Within weeks, everyone loved red beans and rice, crayfish bisque, dirty rice, gumbo, po'boys with just about anything inside, and all kinds of seafood, including raw oysters on the half-shell. Their enthusiasm soon spread to my kids and me.

Although Jewish dietary laws prohibit shrimp, lobster, crab, and oysters, our observance of the rules did not include gustatory denial. Nor were we squeamish Jews, like Woody Allen, widely quoted to have said, "I won't eat oysters. I want my food dead—not sick, not wounded—dead." In my opinion, such picky fanaticism probably lengthened his psychoanalytic treatment. (He would have been better off eating the oysters.)

Not only did we eat everything, we ate them in specific places. It was Bud's for crab, after which we irrigated ourselves with Frosty Freezes from the corner. For beignets and café au lait, it was Café Du Monde or Morning Call. Brennan's was strictly for Sunday brunch and always ended with bananas Foster. It was Casamento's for oyster loaves, the Bon Ton for gumbo and étouffée, and Antoine's (where Dad had a special waiter), Galatoire's, or Commander's Palace for everything else.

Throughout the acculturation of my family, I remained an appreciative outsider on the periphery of their lives, an amused observer of the endless crazy eights games Rick, Ron, and Vicki played, not for money, but for "slavery." The winner's usual demand was a bowl of fresh popcorn, made in a covered pan, shaken back and forth over a gas burner and saturated with melted butter—accompanied by a Coke. Following a debacle of major proportions, a demand for an endless backrub might be added.

I barely knew Perry, the budgie, who lived with them for many years. Perry was boarded every summer when the family made their annual trip from New Orleans to Omaha and Davenport. These were not pleasurable, sightseeing journeys, according to the passengers. Dad, the only driver in the early days, insisted on driving without stopping until it was dark. Once, Rick remembers, he promised they would stop to see the Truman library. True to his word, Dad drove up to the entrance, allowed Rick to enter while he took a picture—and that was the end of the "dilly-dallying."

The cost of boarding Perry each year far exceeded the price they paid for him, but like Hazel, he was considered a member of the family. Perry had an ideal life. He was allowed to fly all over the apartment, except at night, when he was put into his covered cage. Even I could see that Perry had personality.

Mostly he hung out with us in the den. One of his favorite tricks was to scorch the plastic knob at the end of the blinds by exposing it to the lighted bulb in the nearby lamp. He also had keen eye-to-toe coordination. Only the absent-minded or the addled were foolish enough to come into the den barefooted.

When he wasn't with us, Perry loved to perch on the sink in the bathroom, waiting for someone to leave a slightly dripping faucet so he could take his bath. Alas, his predilection to play with water may have played a role in his ignoble end. There is some confusion as to the details, but Perry, unwittingly, was flushed away by a visitor.

There were no more pets, unless you count the snails Vicki kept in her bedroom. The snails had a bad ending too. I happened to walk past the bedroom in time to observe their march to freedom. Forming a perfect line, they climbed up the inside of the bowl, stretched over the edge, descended down the dresser in single file, and disappeared into the netherworld of the carpet below. We never found them.

The duplex turned out to be in a great location. I often walked down St. Charles, enjoying the elegance and charm of the nineteenth century mansions on both sides of the street. Peering past the polished wooden doors through faceted glass to the lighted crystal chandeliers inside, I imagined the warm, gracious lives that took place inside.

Walking down private streets protected by guards, I strolled along the campus of Loyola University until I reached Tulane, where Rick eventually became an undergraduate. Crossing St. Charles, I ambled through Audubon Park, where broad boulevards lined with ancient live oak trees provided dappled shade on hot afternoons. Walking passed the zoo where Vicki, the animal lover, volunteered, I meandered down the quiet lanes that led to the Audubon Golf Course.

Mom and young Rick occasionally played golf there, but more often they played at the country club—until the day Rick lost all of his balls, then lost all of hers, and followed this exhibition by smashing his club into the ground. That did it. She walked off the course, declaring she would never play with him again because of his lack of good sportsmanship. Despite this proclamation, we knew he would worm his way back into her good graces, because he was her favorite, the youngest, and the one who understood her best.

Once in a while, we went shopping on Canal Street.

For these excursions, it was easier to take the streetcar than to hunt for a parking place near this tourist Mecca. We boarded the streetcar at the corner (right outside my bedroom window) and for a dime were rocked gently down to Lee Circle, passed canopied hotels with red carpets and charming specialty shops. Then the gentle rocking stopped and the streetcar turned sharply, lurching its way around the tall column upon which the statue of General Robert E. Lee stood before heading toward Canal Street.

Canal Street was a shopper's paradise. Like State Street in Chicago, it offered a range of merchandise, from novelties to fashion. It also offered a range of shoppers—the elegant, the wannabes, the ones marching to their own drummers, and the ones hoping to pick your pocket. If I were with my brothers, we got off at the schlocky end of Canal Street, where the windows were packed with electronics of all kinds. With my mother, we continued on to the fashionable end, where the department store windows of Maison Blanche, D.H. Holmes, and Gus Mayer beckoned, offering us a glimpse of how stunning we could look if we were willing to buy their upscale merchandise.

Gus Mayer's windows were especially understated and elegant, and that was where Mother liked to shop. She had a personal shopper at the store who called her when something new came in that looked "just like her." After she got to know me, she showed me things that looked just like me. (It is curious that personal shoppers know exactly what looks "just like someone," while that someone has no clue.)

From Canal Street, it was a short walk to Jackson

Square. If the Quarter could be called the heart of the city, Jackson Square was its aorta. Modeled after the Place des Vosges in Paris, Jackson Square was, and still is, a perpetual happening. Throngs of artists and musicians compete with pigeons for space around the statue of Andrew Jackson. It's a self-employed entrepreneur's dream. It's the only place I know where you can listen to jazz, have your picture painted, and your future predicted without moving. And when it all gets to be too much, you can cross the street and have beignets and café au lait at Café Du Monde.

Once he got over the shock of the debacle, my father seemed to have no trouble starting over. He had done it so often in his life, he may have accrued a callus like the shamans who can walk on hot coals. Within weeks of losing his company, he was in New Orleans sorting out his options. After he nailed down his livelihood, he proceeded to build himself a congenial lifestyle.

This turned out to be a matter of one-stop shopping. He had only to join Lakewood Country Club, which was mostly Jewish, to find everything he needed: a compatible golf game and an affable bridge game. It has been widely reported that relationships among men are often based on shared activities. This was definitely true for my father, but his golf game and his bridge game happened to produce life-long friendships. Even though they are all gone, it gives me pleasure to acknowledge them: Jack Levy, "Shep" Shushan, Murrel Kaplan, Sam Rosenberg, Sam Israel, Jessie Rosenfeldt, and especially Jimmy Heymann, my favorite, whose chauffeur used to deliver fresh figs to us at the Nashville apartment.

Starting over wasn't as easy for my mother. She required deeper bonds and a broader spread of emotional sharing. It was hard for her to find that kind of relationship in New Orleans. This was exacerbated by her growing withdrawal. It's hard to pinpoint these things, but I think it began with our move to Oak Park. Each move may have taken her further and further away from her internal sense of home and, perhaps, of her sense of herself. My friend Louise, visiting with me once in New Orleans, observed that the apartment lacked the little touches of an invested life. The tables were bare, she noted, as though Mom could move at the drop of a hat.

I know that my mother yearned for the security of her own place—after all, she was Bobo's daughter—but my father could never be persuaded to buy a house after Oak Park. Even years later, when I bought my first place in Houston, he remained convinced that owning a home would bring certain disaster. "Why would you want to own a house?" he asked, reciting a litany of miseries that occurred during the Depression, all due to foreclosures. (And if he were living through today's real estate debacle, I'm sure he would be reciting the same litany.)

It's possible that my mother was too Midwestern to be comfortable in New Orleans. Through Lakewood, she met a parade of pleasant, somewhat dull women with whom she seemed to have little in common. Once a well-intentioned woman gave a "sherry" party for both of us. Our hostess was careful to provide the names and pedigrees of all her guests to us, but neither of us could remember any of their names or credentials later.

My mother was from the "call a spade a spade" school. Southern gentility was lost on her. She could never reconcile herself to the sharp delineation of classes that she found to be so much a part of the life around her. Despite its French façade, she declared one day, New Orleans was still the South. Having drawn that line in concrete, she dismissed everything south of the Mason-Dixon line.

I, on the other hand, found New Orleans's culture charming, especially Southern men. Dad's friends were so soft-spoken they seemed to wrap their opposing opinions in gauze, the way a diplomatic photographer softens his lens to shoot an aging star. They were so courteous and genteel that, when introduced to my children, they appeared to have nothing more interesting to do than to converse with them at length.

This was a sharp contrast with my Northern male friends, whom I loved dearly, but who were mostly in retail. May I suggest that you never try to have a leisurely conversation with a retailer while his store is open? For a more thorough discussion of businessmen and their obsessions, see *Type A Behavior and Your Heart*, by Herbert Benson.

After Ron, Rick, and Vicki all left New Orleans, Mother's outings became more limited, but she didn't seem unhappy or depressed; in fact, she said her relationship with Dad was better now that they were alone. She may have narrowed her life intentionally. Always a voracious reader, she read the *Times-Picayune* and the *Wall Street Journal* every morning. She read books in the afternoon, as her father had done. She brought home an armful of books from the library every week; a week later, she returned them and picked up another armful.

She was such a familiar visitor to her local branch library, she had a personal shopper there too who stockpiled new books she thought Mom would enjoy. Mysteries and detective stories were her favorites, especially if the book included a trial. She was indiscriminate about Jewish authors. She was intimately familiar with the works of Shalom Aleichem, I.B. Singer, and Bernard Malamud; she even read everything by Norman Mailer. When she wasn't reading, she kept a perennial game of solitaire going or she worked crossword puzzles. If there is a puzzle gene, she passed it on to two generations of avid crossword and sudoku fans.

When her shows were on, there was television to watch. She was a devotee of the soaps, going back to *Oxydol's Own Ma Perkins,* a radio show that dealt endlessly with the indiscretions of Rushville Center. When Ma Perkins disappeared, she turned her attention to *One Man's Family* and *Guiding Light.* Eventually, she moved from impropriety to crime; then it was *Perry Mason* and *NYPD.*

None of these shows interfered with her nightly news programs. Although she watched the news with the fervor of a junkie, she watched only the "sincere" commentators: Walter Cronkite, David Brinkley, and Connie Chung. Once in a while, she watched Barbara Walters, but mainly because she happened to be Jewish—a big plus. In her acidulous opinion, the others were actors—newscasters who read the news but lacked the substance of a real commentator.

Politics became her passion. After her move to New Orleans, she became a born-again liberal, although, Rick said, she never voted after Adlai Stevenson was defeated.

When it came to politics, she was not a dilettante. Incredibly, she seemed to know the voting record of nearly everyone in Congress, particularly the records of those who voted the "wrong way."

Her specialty was the antics of Louisiana politicians. This kept her very busy. "The only kind of politician they won't vote for down here is a boring one," she said to me one day. "In Louisiana, it's more important to be colorful than to be honest." To substantiate this, she cited a list of politicians who had been reelected despite their convictions for various crimes. When I suggested she was finding the shenanigans of Louisiana politics as absorbing as the soaps, she agreed, adding that they were very similar.

I so regret that she did not live to experience the 2008 election. She would have loved it. She would have reveled in Hillary's amazing performance and in Barack's thrilling success. And she would have had unstinting opinions about every shocking detail of corporate greed that has surfaced since then. She would have entertained us all with her judgments, which we now can only imagine.

After I was divorced and the children were grown and gone, it became a ritual for Ron, Rick, and me to spend Thanksgiving in New Orleans with our parents. Sometimes Vicki joined us, sometimes it was Jane, but it was always golf at Lakewood with Dad on Thanksgiving and coming home to the smells of Mother's perfect turkey on Thursday, and it was always golf with Dad on Friday and coming home to the smells of Mother's perfect standing rib roast.

We were such fixtures at Lakewood during Thanksgiving that Jack Levy's greeting was "It must be Thanksgiving if the Schulman kids are here." We were happy with our own foursome. We never wanted to play with anyone else. We knew each other's grooved swings so intimately we could tell when someone began to deviate from the norm. And, because we knew our own swing flaws, we were always experimenting. "How does this look?" one of us would ask the others. "I think I've got it," was practically our family motto. Alas, whatever we "got" never lasted long.

Dad was our steadiest golfer, I came next, and Rick and Ron were our long-ball hitters. In the early days, the boys were all over the place, but as their games improved they began to beat Dad regularly. He must have felt some regret at this loss, but I never saw anything on his face but pride. He was their biggest fan. "Did you see how long that shot was?" he would ask me incredulously.

Despite his Parkinson's, Dad was able to maintain about an eight handicap, give or take a stroke, for many years. Occasionally, he had the fun of playing with a visiting celebrity. Once, I remember, he was paired with Dick Shawn, the comedian, who turned out to be a pretty good golfer; another time he was Arnie Palmer's partner in a PGA member-guest tournament. When he played with Palmer, Rick watched Dad make a birdie on the eighth hole, upon which, Rick said, Palmer grabbed Dad's putter and pretended to try it out, while Jack Levy yelled, "That was little Jew George that made that bird!"

I only remember Dad telling me one story. Once,

he said, when he and his long-time caddy walked past Lakewood's last water hole after a particularly bad round of golf, his caddy turned to him and said, " 'Bout the only thing we didn't do, Mr. Schulman, was throw the clubs in the lake and jump in after them!" That story always made him laugh.

In my prime, I was somewhat better than the average woman golfer, but one fortuitous year I actually won the Davenport Club Championship. When it happened, Dad quipped, "I always knew I sired a champion." This was an especially gracious comment, since he had witnessed so many games when I was the one that should have thrown my clubs into the lake and jumped in after them.

Since Thanksgiving coincided with Mother's birthday, part of our holiday ritual was to shop for her birthday present. This ritual began pleasantly enough, but as we continued to fail to find anything she liked or needed, it became a quest. We tried sweaters, blouses, robes, afghans, handbags, and scarves, but we never came up with a winner.

We had a lot of hope the year we bought her a mini food processor. We were sure she would love "Oskar" because it would put an end to her laborious chopping and dicing into the wooden bowl she had disfigured with vigorous attacks from her primitive chopping tool that resembled a runner from an abandoned ice skate. She agreed to try it, but no matter how gently she pulsed with Oskar, the results were a colorless mush. Oskar became another loser.

When we were still optimistic, we wrapped our gifts

and presented them to her with a flourish. She always thanked us politely, but after the presentation we never saw any of them again. As the years passed, she began to giggle at the very sight of an offering.

Our worst fiasco was the year we presented her with a bonsai plant. Someone got the idea that she might really like this because it fit right into her oriental period. We could imagine it on her Kyoto-style table in the living room, upon which she had placed a miniature Shoji screen. We shopped for possible candidates everywhere, finally selecting a dwarf tree surrounded by miniature shrubs and rocks, tastefully set in a lovely ceramic dish. She took one look at this tiny scene and broke into helpless laughter.

Deciding it was hopeless, we gave up. For her next birthday we went to the nearest hardware store and bought her a deluxe garbage can on wheels. She loved it! Now, she said, Dad could roll the garbage down to the curb without a problem. Who knew?

After Bobo died and left her a small inheritance, Mother became interested in the stock market. Through the years, she managed to parlay her legacy into a handsome estate of her own, giving her a sense of independence that was much too long in coming but which she relished nonetheless. I don't think she ever spent any of her money on herself. In her will, she stipulated that it should all go to her grandchildren.

We have continued the tradition of celebrating Thanksgiving together, although today our participation is much more egalitarian. Everyone cooks, and the menu has greatly expanded to accommodate other families' traditions. We now serve mashed potatoes, a Jell-O mold, tossed salad, two kinds of stuffing, a vegetable casserole, a pineapple dish, two sweet potato casseroles, two cranberry dishes, dinner rolls, and three desserts.

In our quest to produce the perfect turkey, we have covered it with a foil tent, roasted it in a paper sack, roasted it in an oven bag, brined it overnight, and grill-roasted it in a convection oven. Any change in the way "Mom did it" produces an unbelievable spewing of discontent: "I like jellied cranberries right from the can, sliced on a plate like Mom did it." Or, "Why can't we just have sweet potatoes with melted marshmallows, the way Mom made it?"

For the last few years, we have rented beach houses in Galveston for the whole weekend. Long sandy walks have taken the place of golf. When we gather for dinner, the emanating smells are different, but we are still together.

I wish my parents had hung around a little longer. Mother never knew that Rick got married, that Jon and Lori had Alexis, or that Jane married Michael and now has Nathan and Elliot. Dad never knew that Rick and Linda had a daughter, Rebecca, whose bat mitzvah we all celebrated a few years ago. Part of the sadness I feel at their loss comes from knowing how happy these things would have made them. But I'm sure they knew we would continue to be a family and watch out for each other.

Each of my sibs plays a significant and singular role in my ever-evolving life. Ron, the former nudge, continually comes to my rescue, donating his excellent problem-solving skills and considerable muscle to most of my cockamamie projects. Vicki has forgiven me for being the model she couldn't seem to live up to throughout her childhood and has now surpassed me in all of the domestic arts. I consult with Rick on a wide range of topics; so far, I haven't found anything he doesn't know about.

We decided recently it was time to spend a weekend together in New Orleans. It was our first visit there as a family since the folks moved away, and the first since Hurricane Katrina. Although the devastation from the storm could still be seen, particularly in the poorer sections of the city, most of the places where our memories took place were intact. We found all the apartments where the family lived. We checked out Audubon Park, the Quarter, Jackson Square, and Tulane. We had an elegant dinner at Commander's Palace, barbeque shrimp at Pascal Manale's, oyster po'boys at Casamento's, and brunch at Brennan's. We tried to find Lakewood, but not much remained.

Each place we visited evoked happy memories, and each memory led to another until it seemed we had recovered it all. There were no tears. There was music, as rich and infectious as ever; Tchoupitoulas and Melpomene were still there to regale the newcomers; the blend of French, Spanish, Indian, and African influences was still powerful enough to cast its unique spell.

Despite all this, New Orleans will never be the same for us. It will remain linked with the memory and the lives of our parents. There will never be that golf game or the smell of a perfect turkey waiting for us. *Laissez les bon temps roulez* no longer seems appropriate. To me, the city now suggests an aging paramour who has seen better days. I am grateful to have known her in her prime. That is the way I will always remember her.

Santa Barbara, the House on Marianna Way

"Marriage has no guarantees. If that's
what you're looking for,
go live with a car battery."
—Erma Bombeck

According to *Oxford's English Dictionary,* you reach the point of no return when you don't have enough fuel to get back to where you began. That pretty much describes the state of our marriage when Jane, our youngest child, left for college.

It was dramatic. I felt as though my contract had suddenly ended, and I was unemployed. We might have kept our two-track marriage going for a while, but the track I had been following for twenty-five years seemed to have ended in a field of overgrown weeds. Larry's track, on the other hand, was prospering. He closed the little family store on Third Street and opened stores in two new shopping malls. He was now a chain-store operator and a firmly established player in his mother's dream.

I needed to find a new road quickly. Only one seemed to beckon: the fork in the road I didn't take, the last place I felt I was a work in progress with possibilities that stretched to the horizon—academia. Until now, I had taken classes in anything that interested me, the subject didn't have to be useful; in fact, you could say my specialty was useless information. Unless you consider holding my own in dinner party conversations that required only a smattering of knowledge in the fields of philosophy, literature, and the color-field paintings of Jules Olitsky useful, as Ray apparently did.

Relentlessly, which is how I pursue everything, I pivoted 180 degrees and pointed myself in the direction of schools offering income-generating classes that might lead to a job. Trade schools, vocational schools, technical institutes—I perused them all. (I eliminated rabbinical schools, because I was exploring Hinduism, and believed in an internal higher power somewhere near my solar plexus that functioned as my center for Etheric-Psychic Knowing. A lot of congregations can be picky about stuff like that.)

Trying to come up with something—anything—I grappled with what seemed to be the significant questions: What? Where? How? Who? When? (Although I may have confused this with the significant questions suggested by my Journalism 101 textbook.) Since I already had a handle on "who," and I was pretty sure "when" was immediately, that just left, "what," "how," and "where."

I went directly to the you-know-what, skipping the stacks with Proust, Kant, and Julia Child, and headed for Richard Bolles and his classic *What Color is Your Parachute?* The cover of the book proclaimed it was "the bible for career changers seeking fulfillment." Perfect. Fulfillment, for less than twenty dollars. The first chapter said to start with an inventory of my skills. I was in trouble right already. What *were* my skills? Shlepping kids to swimming lessons? Writing skits for Sisterhood? Supervising the construction of a house? That one didn't turn out so well. How about my latest skill, recognizing my feelings and expressing them?

No wonder I got depressed. This was really depressing.

In the end, I choose a professional school that offered a BA degree and training in photography. I wasn't sure I had any talent, but I did have some experience photographing jewelry and setting up tabletop shots for the newspaper ads I put together for the store. And I had a 35-millimeter camera with three lenses. I knew going to a nuts-and-bolts school like this at my age was going to be a challenge—particularly since I scarcely knew the difference between a nut and a bolt—but as my center of Etheric-Psychic Knowledge already knew, even if I didn't have talent, I did had the resolve of a pit bull. I submitted a portfolio to Brooks Institute in Santa Barbara and, to my great relief, I was accepted.

Now I had a direction and a road. All I needed was a major. The classes listed in the catalog offered a plethora of career possibilities: journalism, illustration, portraiture, film, and, at the technical end, industrial photography. Which one should I choose? Let's see, which one offered no chance for creative expression in a field in which I had absolutely no interest? Which one had nothing to offer but the best chance for a job, albeit in an industrial setting, an unfamiliar environment I had only seen in movies?

You probably guessed it. With visions of bag ladies dancing in my head, I chose industrial photography. There might jobs in those other, more touchy-feely fields, but I could see that manufacturers and factories all over the country were actually advertising for people.

Never mind that industrial photography was clearly the most difficult curriculum. Or that I was forty-seven with nothing going for me but a cluster of totally unrelated skills, and this major would add more unrelated skills to the mix—like the ability to take stroboscopic photographs of bullets rupturing an apple and drops of milk refracting and falling into a cup.

I could rationalize my decision by paraphrasing Robert Browning: "A woman's reach should be beyond her grasp, or what's a heaven for?" But who would believe I was influenced by that poetic thought? It was abject fear. The bag lady syndrome. Although I had never really been poor, I was pretty sure I wouldn't like it. And, as my divorce attorney pointed out in my first office visit to him, I was "unmarketable." Even if I wanted one, apparently my prospects for a second marriage were dim. I clearly needed all the help I could get.

I am going to interrupt the flow of my story here because now that the "d" word has been mentioned, you may be wondering if you somehow skipped something. In case you were hoping for something dramatic with prurient details, I thought I would let you know that I have chosen to gloss over the details of our divorce and skip a lot of trauma.

Discretionary omissions like this often occur in films. Directors can choose to fade to black at the end of a scene and resume the story years later, in a different location. Memoirists can do this more subtly. Without fading to black, we can just rummage through our mental files and choose what we want to include in our books. But for the sake of closure, I have rummaged through my life to provide this finale:

Imagine a courtroom scene with a judge, two or three lawyers, and a scraggly bunch of witnesses. The witnesses are there because Larry is contesting our divorce. When it's his turn, he tells the judge he is contesting it because he believes our marriage is still viable. To explain his position, he says that I am his helpmate, his housekeeper, and his social secretary.

Following this, my only witness—our friend Louise, who was gutsy enough to appear on my behalf—takes the stand. She brings up the subject of "irreconcilable differences," which is just another way of describing the point of no return I mentioned earlier. She says she believes it is an accurate description of our marriage, mainly because it is her opinion that we are irreconcilably different.

After hearing all the evidence, the judge decided on dissolution. Despite, she added wryly, the excellent quality of the services associated with the marriage, which Mr. Siegel had mentioned earlier. I ended up accepting the terms of the settlement, although I thought it should have been much more generous, considering the twenty-five years of splendid service I had provided, because I felt so guilty. We sold the house and divided up the furniture. Fade to black.

My moving company agreed to put my things in storage until I had an address in Santa Barbara. I began my odyssey across the country in a newly purchased sky blue

1976 Mercury Comet. It was the first car I ever bought for myself. I paid for it by cobbling together my income from various writing projects, including my copywriting job for a local advertising company and a stint as the public relations director for the local chiropractic college. I even *hondled* for the car. (The closest English equivalent for this word is "bargained," which is water compared to broth.)

Having assisted in my "outing," Louise was adamant about accompanying me to California. Knowing how directionally challenged I am, I think she wanted to make sure I found Santa Barbara. She stayed on the job until I was settled in my apartment on Marianna Way, not too far from the Brooks campus and just a few blocks from the beach. It took us two days to find something that felt right. Luckily, it came with a nice couple willing to rent the other half of their duplex to a middle-aged student with no local recommendations and no discernible income.

My new place was charming. It had cheerful Mexican tile in the entry hall and a sunny kitchen. Just beyond was a large living room and dining room with practical brown carpet. There was even a fireplace and glass doors leading to a tropical plant-filled patio. Upstairs were two bedrooms with a bath in between. From the front guest bedroom, I could see the mountains, and by angling the pier glass in the back master bedroom, I could reflect the view right to my bed. The Pineacre furniture fit perfectly into its new surroundings, and it is all still with me today.

Unfortunately, classes didn't begin for a few weeks. Each day that I spent waiting for my new life to start seemed endless. For the first time in my life, I was alone in an unfamiliar city. No one called, no one came home at the end of the day, and no one asked, "What's for dinner?"

My nightly entertainment was driving the Comet to the beach to watch the sunset. A crowd gathered there every night to see the show. It reminded me of going to a drive-in movie. Some people even brought popcorn. We sat on picnic tables and watched the orange ball drop to the horizon, shrink to a tubular top hat, flatten to an egg yolk, and disappear into an orange ripple. We clapped in appreciation every night.

I would have enjoyed the peace and quiet of that interlude more if I had known what was about to befall me once I started school. Brooks Institute, so charming and friendly in the brochure, might offer a bachelor's degree and some occupational skills that would look good on a resume, but it wasn't going to offer a gentle transition into independence.

Instead of a nurturing climate, it provided boot-camp training. We were welcomed on our first day by the school's "commanding officer." He suggested that we look at the students to our left and to our right. Chances are, he said, we wouldn't be seeing them at graduation two and a half years from now; in fact, he pointed out, since the attrition rate at Brooks was close to fifty percent, we might not be there ourselves.

It didn't take long to see why so many students dropped out. After a day or two, I began to suspect Nazi storm troopers had trained the teaching staff. The slightest infraction of a subtle technicality on a submitted assignment meant all the hours spent producing it were wasted.

"Redo" was the order of the day, which meant more midnight hours in the damp, acerbic processing lab. Making it to the Promised Land of graduation was going to require all the perseverance embedded in my genetic coding. I could only hope that no one in my gene pool had ever unknowingly cohabitated with a hedonist wastrel.

Despite the fact that alarming clusters of purple veins were emerging on my legs from these all-night sessions and that my children were older than most of my fellow sufferers, it never occurred to me to quit. I was determined to acquire the credentials I needed to open those doors to a professional future.

That meant I had to master Industrial Photography. One look at my classmates and I knew I was in trouble. All male, they looked as though they could repair their own cars and maybe build a rocket without instructions. This was going to be like expecting Goldie Hawn to play Hamlet's mother. I had finally gone beyond chutzpah; this was self-flagellation.

Once again I'm going to skip the trauma—the sleepless nights, the constant redos, the frequent calls from my divorce attorney over one thing or another—and the general feeling that I had blundered into the wrong life.

Let's just say that I beat the odds and managed to graduate. I even managed to turn a lemon into limoncello. I still regret that I turned down the chance to make a movie with Ernie Brooks and his submarine because it would have required me to stay in school an extra semester.

But I did write articles and humor pieces for the school newspaper, and I received a special faculty award.

I also made a lot of young friends who often invited me to "boogie" with them on weekends. During the time I lived on Marianna Way, my fellow students shared their secrets (and some of them were doozies), taught me the correct way to smoke marijuana (yes, I did inhale), and sang songs to me on their guitars. They also helped me master the technicalities of my view camera, with its bellows and hood. Once in a while, when we weren't working on a project, we watched the sunset together and talked about the mysteries of life, which now included our own still murky futures.

On the day I graduated, my brother Rick traveled down from Oakland, where he taught and still teaches political science classes at Mills College, to attend the glorious event. I sat in the audience wearing my coveted cap and gown, waiting for my name to be called. While I waited, vignettes of my life flashed through my mind, almost imperceptibly, as though they were projections on the windows of a moving train.

When at last my name was called, I climbed the stairs to a thunderous ovation. When I turned around, I saw that everyone in the room was standing, including the faculty. "Way to go, girl!" someone shouted from the balcony. I blinked back tears. I could never have imagined an ending like this. It had been a long and arduous journey, but I was finally standing on the other side of that fork in the road, which I hoped would lead to financial independence.

Over time, my fears of becoming a bag lady receded, and I stopped sweating over every bill that reached three figures. Despite the ordeal I suffered at Brooks, I did go back to school once more. This time I managed to survive epidemiology and statistics. I even wrote a thesis. The evidence of my master's degree in public health now hangs behind the door in the storage closet I made into an office. My diplomas are only symbols of completion. They don't signify the end of my learning process. I plan to be a work in progress until I see that light at the end of the tunnel. I hope the light leads right to the adult education department. A class called "Merging Your Stroboscopic Photographs and Your Etheric-Psychic Center through the Magic of Photoshop Layers" would be perfect.

Houston, Home Sweet Condominium

"Education is an admirable thing, but it is
well to remember from time to time
that nothing worth knowing can be taught."
—Oscar Wilde

When I graduated from Brooks I was almost fifty, and my resume of gainful employment resembled my grandfather's when he arrived from Petrokov, Russia—before he got the job with the Jewish butcher. Worse, I had run out of scenario for my movie starring me. I had explored everything Richard Bolles suggested in his book. I had credentials. But here I was, facing a blank page. I knew it was time to bite the stroboscopic bullet and find a job, but I didn't feel ready. This stumbling block was beyond the realm of the library. I had to find the answer to the blank page inside. Unfortunately, I had regressed to the "what," "how," and "where" business.

To be honest, I was even having trouble with the "who" part. Fortunately, Santa Barbara, being in the state of California, offered a full complement of workshops designed for "who" seekers. I passed on the workshop that could help me achieve my full sexual potential and the one that offered to regress me back to my earlier lives. I picked one Studs Terkell might have designed. It offered a series of insightful exercises to assist the job seeker in finding meaningful work. According to the exercises, finding meaningful work in my case meant successfully merging my masculine and feminine sides. Now, there were two of us needing a job.

I started my search in San Francisco because I had family living there: My daughter, Julie—who now wished to be known as Ashely, producing a processing glitch for me and a new compound name for her, "Jew-Ash"—and my brother Rick, who also had two names, Paul his preferred professional one, and Rick, his family name. I avoided this mental lapse by never calling him Paul, despite his preference.

Almost overnight, Rick's extra bedroom became my war room: newspapers, phone books, and endless lists appropriated all the available space in the room. There were lists of contacts, lists of prospects, lists from contacts and prospects, all of which I carried with me on job interviews— along with a pen to note comments. The comments I noted were all rejections.

My lists seemed to multiply every day without producing a single job. Rick tried to bolster my spirits with cheerful affirmations every morning before he left for work. These were *a capella* versions of "When You Walk Through a Storm" and "Oh, Happy Day."

They worked for a while. The first few days, I sallied forth with my brand-new, very attractive portfolio case, my lists, and a map. I wouldn't say I attacked the search with gusto; it was more like a pig with a cold hoping to sniff out a truffle anyway. I remained resolute as I passed the shouting crazies who seemed to congregate on every street corner. I marched hopefully into the offices of marketing, advertising, and human resources specialists. The answers were always the same: "good portfolio," "no opening right now," "keeping your information on file." The man at PG&A buffered his rejection by saying I would outgrow anything he could offer me in six months. I labeled this a good example of damning with faint praise.

I tried to keep my spirits up, but my Etheric-Psychic Center was sending me messages that California was not right for me anyway. After a while, I began to listen to these messages. Californians were focused on leisure, playing, and fun on the weekend. What was I focused on? Work, suffering, and making money. Californians were thinking crème brûlée. I was thinking rubbery green Jell-O. Besides, the shouting crazies and the begging street people had begun to freak me out. It was too easy to identify with them. If I didn't find a job soon, I could be right there with them.

To add to my discomfort, it was now 1979, the year of the Iran hostage crisis. In the wake of our deteriorating relationship with Iran, we faced severe gasoline shortages at home. Rationing was instituted. There were long lines at the service stations. We were allowed to fill our tanks only on certain days, depending on the initial letter of our last name. When I left the Elysian Fields of Davenport I didn't realize I would end up in a war zone.

One night Rick came home to find me packing and blubbering. He tried to comfort me, but I was suffering from my own idiosyncratic version of post-traumatic stress syndrome. I left for Santa Barbara the next day, resolved to look anywhere but in California for work—some place where my masculine and feminine sides could merge and allow me to find work, suffering, and money.

I started searching through the Sunday classified sections of various newspapers. One glance at the astonishing number of jobs listed in the *Houston Post* (now defunct) and I heard Circe's call. Not only did Houston have jobs, it would surely have plenty of gasoline, because you could pump it right out of the ground there. Plus, it didn't have distractions like mountains or the ocean. People living in Houston were sure to be focused on work. Or, as one of my leisure-oriented Californian friends put it, "Why else would you live there?"

Best of all, Texas didn't have a state income tax. This was very significant to me, since I was paying income taxes to the state of California on the meager annual distribution I was receiving from my divorce. I called the only two people I knew who lived in Houston: Lois Landa, an old college chum, and Joan Silvers, Larry's cousin. Lois said she couldn't wait for me to come, and Joan immediately offered me the use of her house and car while she and her family went on a two-week vacation. A week later, I flew to Houston.

Joan's house was spacious and comfortable, but there were two small obstacles. Twenty-five years ago, which was the last time I drove a car with a stick shift, there were only three forward gears and a reverse. Joan's car had five gears. What was I supposed to do with the extra one? The other obstacle was feeding the household animals. The dog and the cat were not a problem, but there was also a large rat. It may have been a gerbil, but the subtle differences between these two were indistinguishable to me. Although the animal was in a cage now, I knew it was just a matter of time until it learned to chew through metal and run around the house.

The next morning, I called upon my determination gene, the one I inherited from my father, and once again I sallied forth with my portfolio, a list of prospects, and a map. This time, I also kept the owner's manual, open to the gearshift page, next to me on the front seat. My list of prospects in Houston was limited to one yellow page of the telephone book, under the listing "Multimedia," but I never needed more than the top two listings.

By the time Joan and her family returned from their two-week vacation, I had a job—and I had bought a condominium. It's shocking that it all happened in two weeks, but my purchase was not exactly out of the blue: psychologically I needed roots and financially I needed deductions and they came together when I saw just the right place. Lois, now functioning as a precursor to Google, guided me through this process. She knew the territory; in fact, she and her family were living in the territory—in a bigger version of my new condo. Later, she facilitated my social life by introducing me to all her friends who became my friends—another example of the Jewish tzimmes thing.

My new home was a two-story condominium in the middle of an apartment complex protected by gates and brick walls, and less than a mile from the Galleria and Saks. It came with a homeowners' association that managed the upkeep of the grounds and maintained my exterior. For the first time since I had left Iowa, I felt I was home—a home I bought without considering anyone's needs but my own.

The condo had two bedrooms and a bath upstairs, an arrangement similar to my place on Marianna Way, but no amount of manipulation could summon up a view of the mountains. It didn't have a fireplace downstairs either, but there was a powder room, a good-sized L-shaped living room and dining room, a walled-in patio, and a two-car garage with a carport beyond. My furniture from Davenport fit perfectly everywhere. Things were coming together.

Except for my new job. It began to fall apart shortly after I started. The company that had appeared so friendly and so warm during my interview was a partnership. Unfortunately, one of the partners turned out to be an alcoholic whose idea of meaningful work was to assault his partner with verbal attacks whenever he could think of one. These attacks took place behind closed doors in the beginning, but as his hostility accelerated, this nicety was forgotten. A month later, the abused partner hired a lawyer and struck off on her own.

This left me with a collection of very odd coworkers. There was the alcoholic; another writer who had two or three long-time accounts and spent most of his day chain-smoking in the alcoholic's office; an artist whose passion was drawing cars with flames licking up the hood; and an assortment of technicians whose talents I couldn't discern because they were on the phone a lot.

It was not an auspicious start, but to coin a phrase I just made up, even an onion can turn into chopped liver. Plum projects, booked by the former partner when she was with the company, began to show up on my desk.

These were multimedia shows for major corporations with big budgets. They probably landed on my desk by default because no one knew what to do with them. I didn't know what to with them either, but I had been throwing myself into things I didn't know how to do for years. Soon I was writing scripts, designing visuals, and conferring with the department heads of these huge companies without a lick of experience.

This should have made me happy, but I was miserable. The company was a complete disaster. The atmosphere was radioactive. You could feel the emission of ionizing particles. To top it off, I had an uneasy feeling that the alcoholic was grooming me for his former partner's position. One night, as I was sniffling into a Kleenex and mulling over my nonexistent options, the telephone rang. If a screenwriter had the chutzpah to write a scene about what happened next—after showing a despairing heroine sniffling into her Kleenex—the movie would be so unbelievable the entire audience would stand up and demanded its money back.

Yet, as unbelievable as it may seem, the call was from one of my plum clients offering me a wonderful job. It was all so timely, so fortuitous, it reminded me of my grandfather's story about the wired money that mysteriously arrived in China in the nick of time. It left me ruminating over those same unanswerable questions that occupied us on those dark nights in front of the fish market.

With my new job, I went from the ridiculous to the

sublime. I was now working for a nonprofit organization located in a lovely building surrounded by a grove of trees and landscaped with walking trails. An upscale spa shared the property. And it was all just ten minutes from my new house.

Every morning, I swept into my office doing my best wannabe Loretta Young impersonation. Loretta's weekly television show always began with a shot of her sweeping through her office door, elegantly dressed in long twirling skirts, perfect makeup, and scrupulously coiffed hair. I don't remember what she did that required such sartorial splendor. In my humbler version, I swept through the door in a tailored suit and a pixie haircut.

I was impressed to learn that my new organization had a lofty mission statement. Its purpose was to increase productivity in American corporations by implementing the Japanese approach of participative management. How esoteric, how thrilling to be part of a movement to change American management's autocratic style—and how right up my democratic alley! My colleagues now were a collection of well-educated specialists in education, business administration, the law, and program design. It was, to use an overworked term now applied to everything from lipstick to open-heart surgery, but perfect in this case—awesome!

I even had a title, "Media Development Manager." That's what it said on my brand-new cards, but it was a grandiose description. I only managed one recently graduated technician. This experience was enough to convince me that I never wanted to manage anyone again. My staff person had an unfortunate, and I assume absent-minded, habit of stuffing his thumb and index finger up his nostrils when he was deep in thought. I found this so disgusting that I avoided looking at him whenever possible. Discussing his performance with him was out of the question.

With the exception of this small aberration, I was surrounded by such elegance I couldn't wait to come to work every day. I should have known it was all too good to last. The boom that characterized Houston's economic growth in the 1970s—which had brought me here—cratered in the 1980s. In addition to the national recession, the oil market began to fluctuate wildly. Abruptly, the needle measuring the city's major industry, petrochemicals, swung to "bust."

As a nonprofit organization dependent on the support of corporations, which wasn't happening, all jobs not contributing directly to its bottom line had to be eliminated. This included mine. Instead of Loretta Young, I was suddenly Cinderella before the ball. Instead of holding seminars for CEOs, we were now holding outplacement seminars for our own employees. And these seminars were not offering touchy-feely insights about merging our masculine and feminine sides. They were offering practical advice, like how to file for unemployment.

I was in the process of updating my resume when an old friend who also happened to be a savvy businessman came to visit. "This is why our people go into business for themselves," he pointed out. "Why not try it? What have you got to lose?" When no writing or photography jobs appeared in the classified section for several weeks, I drew up the papers and declared myself a sole proprietor.

With this declaration, I went into a frenzy of activity. I went to the library, I joined professional groups, I created marketing materials, I networked, I compiled videos of every show I had ever written and produced. When the frenzy subsided, I made a list and forced myself to cold-call possible clients. Once I got over feeling like Willy Loman in *Death of a Salesman,* I realized I was actually enjoying it all. Was this my latent masculine side, with a sudden urge to merge?

I tried to schedule two appointments a day. I never knew whom I would meet and what I would learn. I found it amazing what people did for a living, especially in Houston. I called on successful companies that manufactured flanges, bulkheads, and tankless water heaters. I met service providers that bent tubes, detected leaks, and remediated mold.

When my first client said yes, I went into shock. Like the tea parties I held in Bobo's attic, all my effort had gone into preparation. I hadn't even considered what I would do when I finally made a sale. I wasn't sure I was ready, but I had just become "DBA Donna Siegel Communications," ready or not. With that thought spurring me into action, I drove to an office supply store and bought a ledger. I looked at the expandable files labeled cash flow, receivables, taxes, and deductibles, but I bought a file cabinet I wouldn't outgrow when the need for additional labels showed up.

It was thrilling to discover how easily I was able to put my client's full-scale marketing piece together practically alone. I was the writer, the photographer, the producer, and the director. I hired a sound engineer and a professional narrator and managed to create the video, complete with soundtrack and music, in a week. Everything flowed together. I'd like to credit my Etheric-Psychic Center, but I know it came from writing all those cockamamie skits.

I never got over the joy of creating something from nothing. I broadened my scope to include writing articles and essays for various corporate entities. Eventually, my client list included oil service companies, banks, public utilities, and a number of small companies.

Sometimes these projects led to unexpected experiences. An article about life on an oilrig for an oil services company gave me a rare opportunity to participate in the ongoing, robust life aboard one of these behemoth structures. Another time, a proposal I wrote for the University of Houston was funded by the Department of Labor, and later became my master's thesis.

Reflecting this now, I can characterize my entire career as a series of serendipitous events, just one happenstance after another. It would have been much easier to become a dentist. Dentistry follows a discernible track on a major highway. I followed the meandering two-lane roads William Least Heat-Moon wrote about in *Blue Highways*. But in my own circuitous way, I got there. I managed to plumb the mysteries of cash flow, receivables, taxes, and deductibles. My masculine and feminine sides learned to work together so well, they fused. Now I can't tell one from the other.

The twenty-five years I lived in my condo reflected this internal change. When I moved in, everything was either Harvest Gold or Avocado Green, the colors of the period. Green ivy twined around yellow cups down the kitchen wallpaper. In the powder room, delicate gold flowers climbed the green walls. In the living room, gold brocade drapes covered the sliding glass doors, effectively shutting out nearly all the natural light. The effect was sobering. It could have been a grand ballroom in reduced circumstances, or an intimate funeral parlor before the coffin was rolled in.

I redecorated in increments, as I grew more comfortable about the bag lady thing. When I sold my condominium, the walls were taupe, the carpet was white, translucent vertical shutters covered the windows and the sliding door, and there were built-ins and books everywhere. There was nothing more to do. I had to move.

I was the first of my family to move to Houston, but over the years, other family members have come to write new chapters to their own stories. My daughter, Jane, was first. Then came my son Jon and his wife Lori. They were followed by my brother, Ron. Finally, my daughter Ashely, moved here. My parents came too, but their book was pretty much written by the time they moved here. Instead of writing a new chapter in Houston, they wrote their last one here.

My father's Parkinson's disease remained relatively benign into his late seventies. He could drive, spend a few hours in the office, play bridge, and meet his friends for eighteen holes of golf. But the disease advanced from one tremulous hand to his legs. Teeing up his golf ball one day, he lost his balance and fell over. Frightened and embarrassed, he left the golf course and drove himself home.

Some time later, he fell down the steep stairs of their apartment. Not long after that, he took a bath and couldn't get himself out of the tub. Mother tried to help him. They struggled for hours. That was it. Mother gave up for both of them. Moving them to Houston seemed logical: I was their oldest daughter, Houston winters were mild, and the city offered a range of housing options, from gracious retirement apartments with amenities rivaling a good hotel to Seven Acres, the Jewish nursing home.

Ron flew to New Orleans from Chicago and took care of everything. He sold or gave away everything they wouldn't be taking with them. I investigated the housing options in Houston. Although my father was using a cane at the time, we knew he would progress to a walker in the near future. A walker, we soon discovered, was the dividing line that separated "independent" from "assisted" living in these facilities. We settled on the assisted living section of a cheerful retirement complex, nicely landscaped with ponds and fountains and plenty of group activities for those who were interested. It was clear from the beginning my parents would not be interested. They took one look around them and declared the other residents to be "very sick." Everyone, they said, was in far worse shape than they were. Certainly in my mother's case, they were.

Their new apartment was smaller than any space they had ever shared. It had a living room with an efficiency kitchen at one end, a bedroom, a tiny study, and one luxurious touch—two bathrooms. Every room had an emergency cord. Although the apartment was furnished with their things from New Orleans (the Baker couch, the oriental appointments), nothing looked right here. Neither did my parents.

Dad's health continued to deteriorate. Their loss of personal freedom exacerbated the situation. Their frustration with each other escalated. Having lived away from them for years, I had forgotten how difficult it was to witness these outbursts. I was also struggling with the demands of my own life. I was now working, going to graduate school, and writing my thesis. I felt guilty wherever I was and whatever I was doing. I knew I was failing them. They were miserable, but I didn't know how to make their lives better. Fortunately, Jane was living in Houston by then. She was working, but not yet married. She visited them whenever she could, and willingly took over their finances. They brightened at the sight of her.

As my father became incontinent and began to hallucinate, my mother lost the last vestiges of her own independence. Always a reliable record keeper, she couldn't remember if she had paid the bills that had stacked up in the study. She worried about her memory. Was it Alzheimer's? I knew she was very depressed. In addition to her emphysema, she suddenly developed high blood pressure.

The events of the next few weeks are hazy. Dad's doctor suggested a short hospitalization without medications, which he called a "drug holiday." He hoped this would jump-start the effectiveness of Dad's drugs and reduce their side effects. After his hospitalization, Dad was taken to a rehab center for occupational therapy. Finally, we admitted him to Seven Acres. There was no other choice.

We found a cheerful apartment close to Seven Acres for Mother. She liked the apartment, but living alone for the first time in her entire life was a difficult adjustment. Despite my father's shortcomings, he had been the organizing principle of her life for over sixty years. What was she supposed to do now?

But she was a trouper. When she realized the residents of her apartment complex were mostly her age and Jewish, she agreed to attend an open house. She even accepted an invitation to play bridge. The man living next door, whose wife was also a resident of Seven Acres, began to call her almost daily, offering her rides, asking to borrow her vacuum cleaner, finding numerous other reasons to ring her bell. Mother began to exhibit some rusty but not forgotten social skills.

The drug holiday did not improve Dad's condition. When he was moved to the rehab facility, he lay in his bed speechless and uncomprehending for days. Either Ron or Rick thought of bringing him earphones and a Pavarotti tape, remembering that Dad had often said a voice like Pavarotti's comes once in a lifetime.

We hooked him up and started the tape, all of us taking positions around the bed, searching his face for a sign that life was still pulsing somewhere within his frozen, lifeless exterior. As we watched, a single tear appeared in the corner of one eye and began a slow journey down his cheek.

None of us have forgotten that moment. On the day Pavarotti died, excerpts of him singing "Nessun Dorma" from Puccini's *Turodot* played repeatedly on television. Whenever we heard it, we all relived that scene. Even today, I never hear Pavarotti's voice without thinking about that tear—the symbol of Dad's reawakening.

When we moved Dad to Seven Acres, he couldn't understand why he wasn't going home with Mom. Still, he liked living there. He loved the Yiddishkeit of it all, the daily services, the kosher meals, and most of all the rabbi. He thought he was living in a large Jewish hotel. He soon settled into a daily routine, which included going to services every morning.

Dad had an abiding philosophy that persisted throughout his life, from his Russian childhood to his last days in the nursing home. He believed that any adversity could be overcome by willpower, especially his willpower—and, by extension, ours. "Where there's a will, there's a way," we heard repeatedly through our childhoods. If we remained unconvinced, he was ready to follow up with, "Necessity is the mother of invention."

Not only did he believe this, at Seven Acres he provided us with proof. There was a house rule at Seven Acres that all residents in wheelchairs had to be strapped to their chairs for safety reasons. Dad accepted the fact that he had to be in a wheelchair, but he refused to be strapped down. Each time the nurses tried, he found a way to get loose. They finally gave up, calling him "the Houdini of Seven Acres." Later, when he discovered he could walk by pushing his chair down the hall in front of him, they didn't try to stop him. He became a familiar sight in the halls, steering himself to physical therapy, to the lunchroom, to morning services.

He loved the services at Seven Acres. The rabbi, he said, was what a rabbi should be. He was *frum* (pious), steeped in religiosity, like a strong cup of tea. It didn't hurt that the rabbi had an incredible voice—not showy, but so beautiful and so full of feeling that Dad was often moved to tears. Dad brought his own prayer book to services at first, but they were using a different version. When he realized their pages were totally different, he stopped using a book. He knew the prayers by heart anyway. The daily minion requires a quorum of ten men with at least one Kohayn or Cohen, a member of the tribe of priests. Dad became the resident Kohayn almost immediately. If he didn't show up on his own, someone came to fetch him.

But when they wanted to give him an aliyah, the honor of reading a passage from the torah, he always refused. He said people in wheelchairs weren't supposed to read from the torah. He insisted that to read from the torah, you were supposed to be "whole." Although everyone tried to tell him there were different interpretations about this now, no one could dissuade him. To him, religious precepts should not be subject to interpretation—they should remain uncompromising.

Despite his advancing Parkinson's, during the three years he lived in the nursing home, there were times when his voice would regain its former power. When I heard that rich familiar sound sailing over the room, I imagined it was his undefeated spirit soaring beyond the reaches of his frail body. "Where there's a will, there's a way," the Houdini of Seven Acres continued to insist from his wheelchair. But his body failed to receive the message.

During my mother's final visits with my father, I watched them reach out to each other. Sitting close to each other, holding hands, they seemed to find a lot to talk about. No longer responsible for him, my mother felt free again. She began to laugh more, even making him laugh. Something was stirring between them, something that had managed to survive their complicated relationship but tragically could not be expressed until now.

Ironically, my mother died first. Just a few weeks into

her promising new life, she developed an aneurysm and was gone overnight. Shock mingling with pain, the family assembled to break the news to Dad. He was devastated. Weeping bitterly, he mourned her. He expressed his sorrow for all the ways he had failed her, for all that she had missed in life, for the things he could not change, for the money he had amassed at the end of their lives that she had never enjoyed.

The shock of her death seemed to jolt him back into himself. He rarely hallucinated in those later years. To our amazement, he began to exhibit a new, nurturing aspect of his personality. Had he been suppressing this side of himself all along? Or was he trying, consciously or unconsciously, to infuse some of our mother's gentle, compassionate nature into his more stoic one, in an attempt—as he once said—to be both mother and father to us.

I know it would have pleased my mother. I'm sorry she missed it.

Epiphanies from the 18th Floor

"My parents didn't want to move to Florida,
but they turned sixty and that's the law."
—Jerry Seinfeld

The nautilus must grow faster than I do. It seems to take me twenty-five years to grow enough to need a bigger space. That's how many years I was married and how many years I lived in my condo before I moved to this high-rise. But I have stopped counting years. I am counting lifetimes. So far, I have completed three: Before Marriage, During Marriage, and After Marriage. These titles may not be punchy, but their designations are clear. What do generic titles like Eat, Pray, and Love really tell you?

I am now in my fourth lifetime. My working title for this one is "Reaping." I am still full of unsolicited thoughts for future cockamamie projects, but they are stacking up in the wings waiting for me to finish this book. When I began writing it, I was considered a "young old," and writing a family history was an appropriate developmental task for someone in my age group.

Until I went to graduate school, I didn't realize

appropriate tasks came with developmental stages. If I had known I would be given a whole developmental stage to ruminate over my life, I wouldn't have wasted so much time doing it in earlier stages.

I don't think the word "young" is in my job description anymore, but I'm not going to check. Since my internal sense of self has never aged—she is still jitterbugging with Frank Nicholson on the stage of Senn's auditorium—I prefer the more timeless, gracious, French designation, "a woman of a certain age."

When you attain timelessness, developmental tasks are pretty much over. It's a good thing, because I'm getting a lot of flack from my family, who point out that Margaret Mitchell wrote *Gone With the Wind* in much less time than it's taking me to finish this book. One of these detractors recently told me he doesn't believe there *is* a book.

Kierkegaard famously observed, "Life must be lived forwards, but it can only be understood backwards." Kierkegaard was absolutely right. I have been looking backward for years now, and eventually understanding did come. Unfortunately, and no one is sorrier than I am to have to admit this, understanding did not bring wisdom. Having reached the high-rise of life, I would have liked to pass along the gift of wisdom as my parting shot. Regrettably, all I have to offer are a few disparate musings that occurred to me while I wrote this—nothing high enough on the Richter scale to be considered wisdom. Skimpy as they might be, I decided to put these leftover observations in this section because they didn't fit in anywhere else. I am calling them "epiphanies," even though the word has a Christian connotation, because it sounds wiser.

Epiphany #1: The houses about which I have written here may have disappeared from the face of the earth, but they have remained perfectly preserved in my mind, leashed and waiting for their next outing. The "me" I was then is still there too, cutting things out of catalogs in the Lake Street house, roller skating in the fish market, lighting the space heater in the basement apartment in Iowa City, and setting the table in the Pineacre house. I have managed to go one step further than the nautilus: not only am I carrying around all those old houses, I'm still living in them.

Epiphany #2: Some people don't like growing older, but this is a wonderful stage of life for me. Reaching it is a crowning event, similar to that consummate moment when, having prepared a sumptuous dinner, you can finally sit down to enjoy it. That's why I think of this lifetime as "Reaping"—and on occasion, "At Last." After nearly eight decades on the road, I have learned to be the rider. I could tell when it happened by the comfortable, elasticized waistbands that were proliferating in my closet. They proliferated because I have taken myself out of the game. That would be the "acquisition" game, the "adornment game," the "package yourself" game, and the "keep-working-on-your-flaws" game.

I think I am a work in progress on this point: I may be evolved enough to wear purple with red, and white after Labor Day, I don't. And I wear Easy Spirits, but I still lust for the stilettos I regretfully pass at Nordstrom's.

Epiphany #3: I have adjusted to the fact that my life didn't turn out the way it was supposed to: Hollywood never needed a Jewish Shirley Temple; I didn't grow long legs and become a beauty queen; I married the prince, but we didn't live happily ever after; I kept Dr. Spock on the night table by my bed and tried to follow his advice, but my children never voted me "Mother of the Year" for any year in which I would have been eligible. (But there were years I wouldn't have awarded them "Best in Show," either.)

Does anyone's life turn out the way he or she imagines it? Did Octavia imagine that Marc Antony would end up with Cleopatra? Did Marie Callas imagine that Aristotle Onassis would up and marry Jacqueline? When Elizabeth Taylor was picked to star in *National Velvet*, did she think she would marry eight times?

Maybe my life would have turned out differently if my parents had given me career counseling instead of tap-dancing and piano lessons, but I doubt it. Women in my generation were programmed to believe that marriage should be our only career goal, because the prince was coming, and he would be bringing income. Of course he would be Jewish, or else he wouldn't be a prince. I was only eighteen when my prince showed up and he was only nineteen. We were married a year later. What were we thinking? The moral of this story is clear: we should have waited and caught the next developmental stage.

Epiphany #4: Speaking of men—I feel I have to speak of them because they were such as major part of my life—there were four significant ones and a bunch of temps. The significant ones were all different from one another, but they had one thing in common: they were all Republicans. Since I am a bleeding-heart liberal, carrying on my mother's legacy, I can't help but wonder how this could have happened. Did I unwittingly emit a high-pitched signal that could be received only by right-wing conservatives?

I dismissed this thought because the first significant Republican in my life was my father. That was a big surprise, because back then I didn't know Jews could *be* Republicans. I credit him for being very discreet about his opinions—at least at home—especially after my mother became a female Ralph Nader without the political ambition.

Of course, the prince was a Republican. I tried proselytizing him, but when that didn't work, I resigned myself to canceling out his vote. I am proud to say that however touched he may have been after Nixon's "Checkers" speech, I was able to persuade him not to send a supportive message, which many of our staunch Republican friends did. (This is an aside, but have you ever noticed how often Republicans are described as "staunch," while Democrats are referred to as "yellow dogs"? Do you think that's fair?)

I was smart enough not to marry the next Republican in my life. Quite the opposite of my father and the prince, he was neither elegant nor schooled in the art of opening car doors. He was craggy country, an intriguing mixture of scientist and poet, with just the right skills to guide me through the scary post-divorce tsunami I had to conquer to reach my goal of emotional independence.

He knew amazing things. Taking a walk with him

was to discover the ecological mysteries of a balanced environment. Then, one idyllic day, like the serpent beckoning in the Garden of Eden, he said something like, "Unions are choking the life out of American Enterprise." I froze. Could a man with the soul of a poet be staunch? I thought of Wallace Stevens, my favorite poet, who sold insurance and was very staunch. Obviously, he could. I tried to avoid the subject of politics after that, but it was like trying not to touch a cold sore once you know it's there.

He did give me one unforgettable piece of advice that I cherish. It was during those tumultuous days when I continually fretted about my uncertain future. He said, "Don't try to write your book. Allow yourself to read it." I wasn't even trying to write a book then. Although it's practically impossible for an obsessive-compulsive like me to follow such a Zen-like koan, just recalling it can make me smile—and sometimes I even scratch off one thing on my list.

Having attained my current chronological and developmental stage, you would think I would have developed a nose for sniffing out these guys—even a pig develops a nose for a truffle. Yet, once again, I find myself with a lovely man whose only character flaw is his staunchness. Phil Flowers is a delightful companion, and he offers the no-strings, nonjudgmental relationship you read about in self-help books. He opens doors, stands up when I leave the table, and, despite his recent stroke, he can still remember the names of old movie stars whose names elude me, like Nina Foch and Maria Ouspenskaya. Since he was born and raised in Mississippi, I've come to think of him as a "geographic" Republican. In the South, conservatism may be an environmental affliction that affects both parties—look at the Dixiecrats and the Boll Weevil Democrats.

Despite my complaints about the politics of these significant men, each one made a major contribution to my sense of myself as a woman, and they all came into my life just when I needed them. I am grateful to them all. More grateful to some than to others, but as R. Buckminster Fuller once said, "There is nothing in a caterpillar that tells you it's going to be a butterfly." To which I add, "or vice versa."

Epiphany #5: Because of the demands of my inner muse—and the Schulman proclivity for solitude—I have always thought of myself as a loner with good social skills. I have changed my mind on this. Without the relationships I write about here, my life would have been thin, watery gruel. These substantive friendships have enriched my life, nourished my soul, and turned gruel into glorious gumbo.

I have been fortunate enough to acquire good relationships throughout my peripatetic life, sometimes even carrying them along with me into my next reincarnation. I am not taking credit for this. It could be that the fish happened to be biting when I threw out my hook. My friendships have varied from simple one-cell amoebic connections based on a common interest to more complicated four-chambered relationships in which I became highly invested. There were times when a good friend rose to the level of best friend and, more rarely, to the heights of soulmate.

Natalie was my first soulmate. She was also my first

Chicago friend, the one who rescued me from invisibility at Nettelhorst. She was warmly engaging and round, with a heart-shaped face, dark eyes, and long black hair. She was outwardly funny and innately wise—you could even say preternaturally wise, mainly because I just looked it up and it fits.

She lived on Cornelia, on the other side of Broadway, just a few blocks away from our place on Belmont. I liked to go to her apartment after school because there was always something going on there. Also, she had a grand piano in the living room and a Jewish songbook with many songs in C major, which meant very few sharps or flats to remember. I would play these songs over and over, accompanying myself quietly but passionately in a tremulous voice, trying to sound like Aunt Elsie.

Natalie's household was much more interesting than mine. At the top of the list was Natalie's mother, who would drift in and out of the living room, deliver a tangential monologue that never seemed to be directed toward anyone in particular, and ask if we wanted a snack. She was usually carrying their little black dog, Desire, who seemed to live on her hip. I think the dog acquired his unusual name so he could be introduced to guests as "the street cur named Desire," but I don't know whose idea it was. In their household, it could have been any of them.

Also living there was her mother's sister, Aunt Em, a gentle soul with a wandering eye, who was so thin she might have been anorexic, and Natalie's father, who was rarely home when I was there but was a lively presence when he showed up. I couldn't get over how willing he was to drive us anywhere Natalie wanted to go, anytime she wanted to go there. This would never happen in my house. My father did not do errands.

Natalie's cocky brother, Marshall, was a sailor off fighting World War II. When he came home on leave, he usually brought state-of-the-art, long-playing 78-rpm records of big band music, called V-Discs, with him. Servicemen overseas got these free. I learned to dance with Marshall, listening to these "V" (for Victory) discs of Glen Miller songs—"Moonlight Serenade," "In the Mood," "Doin' the Jive," and one called "Annie's Cousin Fanny," which I don't think withstood the test of time.

Out of this somewhat feisty environment, Natalie grew up knowing she wasn't going to sit around waiting for some prince. She was going to be a writer. While my high school education was focused on mastering the subjects of dating and being popular, Natalie was reading short stores and writing some of her own. She was light years ahead of me in depth and intelligence, but some enigmatic connection glued us together. We shared every waking thought, and we had enough of these to empower an hour-long nightly phone call after being together all day.

Nothing was beyond our consideration. Did God exist? If so, was God omnipotent or subject to the laws of nature? Were our lives already foretold? Would we fall in love? How would we know it was the real thing? And, less profound but of great importance, would someone ask us out this weekend?

As close as we were, by the end of high school, our internal scripts were moving us in different directions. The sorority I chose to join at Senn had the most sophisticated girls; Natalie's sorority had more honor students. She became the salutatorian of our class; I had the lead in the senior play. She went to Brandeis and became a member of its first graduating class; I went to the University in Iowa City and, in less than a year, married Larry.

She was the maid of honor at my wedding. We managed to keep track of each other for many years. She got her PhD, taught philosophy, and wrote books. I got an MRS and had three children. (Wasn't this a movie with Shirley MacLaine?)

My Davenport friendships were more enduring. They began shortly after Larry and I were married. In that mysterious, intuitive way in which social groups are formed, three other recently married couples gravitated to us. Without benefit of consanguinity, the eight of us became each other's family. We were the Davises, the Waxenbergs, the Greenswags, and the Siegels. One magnet pulling us together was that we shared an outrageous, often bawdy sense of humor. The things we found funny are beyond the scope of this book and certainly beyond the realm of good taste.

Despite the fact that we four women were all alpha dogs and occasionally drove each other nuts, we became the Ya-Ya Sisterhood before Rebecca Wells was even born. We knew everything about each other, including some secret indiscretions, which we swore never to tell anyone, even when we were in the nursing home—in case we could still remember them.

We were big on celebrating everything. This included pregnancies, nursery school graduations, carpal tunnel surgery, and tubal ligations. For special birthdays, we went all out. We plotted surprise train trips, arranged limousines to offbeat places for dinner, announced our ages on hotel marquees, and once at the track in Chicago a well-connected husband surprised his wife, and the rest of us, by having a race named for her.

We did not ignore our husbands' special birthdays; in fact, these celebrations had a way of becoming elaborate productions. We roasted one of our more colorful husbands by writing parodies about him to all the *Jesus Christ Superstar* songs. Then we hired a local pianist and cut a record of us singing them.

Encouraged by success of this project, we decided to make a movie for the next husband. To cut down on production costs, we wrote, filmed, and edited the movie ourselves. Things were going so well, we decided to add a soundtrack. To make our movie more interesting, we segued a few farfetched digressions into our unsuspecting subject's life story and convinced a sizable number of friends to dress in costumes and disguises and play various roles. We were still editing the night before his birthday, but it was safely in the can minutes before the cast began to assemble to yell, "Surprise!" Our celebrant was speechless, possibly for the first time in his life.

One year we actually talked our conservative, recalcitrant husbands into competing in a citywide costume party. We dresses as the various characters in the *Wizard of Oz*. The lion and the scarecrow had a relatively easy time of it, but the tin man, encased in a spray-painted metal can that extended past his torso, needed help whenever nature called—and, since he drank a lot, it called frequently. We were not surprised to win first place. Who else would go to the lengths we would?

My favorite caper was the time we were invited to a Roaring Twenties party. After a lengthy debate, we decided to rent top hats, tails, and mustaches and appear as various versions of Charlie Chaplin. To make our entrance more dramatic, we created a car out of a long box that formerly held a couch. It was just big enough to hold all of us, and as the *pièce de résistance*, we made headlights for it. That was our swan song.

We four women could never have dreamed back then that our lives would have turned out the way they did. All four of us eventually went to work, two went to graduate school, two wrote books, and one ran a citywide organization. Later, two of us divorced, three were widowed, two remarried, three faced life-threatening illnesses—and one of us has died. Only one of us still lives in Davenport.

We who are left continue to acknowledge each other's birthdays, but now we send cards and donations to our favorite charities. We have mellowed. We don't end each other's sentences anymore, and we try not to interrupt each other's stories, even though we may have heard them all many times. As Linda Loman said, "Attention must be paid." She was referring to her husband, Willy, in *Death of a Salesman*, but we have extended it to include sixty-year-old friendships. To Jeannie, no longer with us, to Norma, and to Louise—thanks for making my life mocha almond fudge.

Of course, there were many other friends from those days, but I'll just name two. Harriette Freeman was my dear friend and frequent "arts and culture" traveling companion. To stand in front of a painting listening to Harriette's explication of the work we contemplated was to experience the confluence of my left and right brains—

she was that good. She is gone now, but I live in a lavish cocoon of her gifts. Paintings, photographs, and art pieces given to me over my lifetime are everywhere. This is a perfect example of why I will never really succeed in living in a sleek, streamlined space.

My relationship with Kay Bucksbaum began during her brief but memorable life in Davenport. One highlight of this time was our weekly class with Mme. Landsman, who spoke Parisian French—and probably could speak Parisian Yiddish too. Kay and I, and a few other highly unrealistic students, organized the class with the hope of polishing our rusty conversational French. Our weekly task was to write and present something in French to the others.

The only one of these presentations I still remember was Kay's. She and a friend had been touring France and her more fluent friend was making all the arrangements. One day Kay pointed out that she was capable of ordering tickets for the event they planned to attend that evening, whereupon she got in the ticket line and requested two tickets from the ticket agent. When nothing happened, she requested two tickets again, a little louder this time. In the pause that followed, her friend ventured, "Kay, if you'll permit me, you are standing there saying, 'God! God!' " (If you know French, you know how easily the two words can be confused.)

Another highlight of Kay's time in Davenport was the year our Passover Seder included matzo balls that stubbornly stuck to the spoon as though bonded there with Krazy Glue. Somewhere I have a picture of all of us standing around a spoon from which a matzo ball dangles. We ate them anyway. I have kept the recipe Kay sent me soon after this event. She entitled it "Matzo Balls for Those Who Like Them Light."

Kay left Davenport long before I did, but she has remained a special friend. In addition to her ability to produce matzo balls that don't stick to the spoon, she recently published her first book, a memoir of her Iowa childhood.

When I moved to Houston I was all about work, but with the arrival of my first Jewish holiday there, Lois Landa bestowed upon me a trove of riches: her collection of close friends who had been celebrating every major Jewish holiday together for so long, they could tell each other jokes by the number. I was destined to be an outsider of Nettelhorst proportions, but I happened to mention that I was reading a book about guiding autobiography groups for older adults. Within weeks, a subset of Lois's friends and I formed a support group, based on the book. We hoped it would comfort and sustain us through the inevitable losses we knew were ahead.

We followed the process described in the book to the letter: we wrote short, two-page essays on the topics suggested and read them aloud to each other at monthly meetings. It was amazing. Even those who had known each other for years, learned things about each other that they never knew. Several of our group have kept their essays and plan to leave them to their children and grandchildren when they are gone.

During our years together, our support group has been severely tested. Our numbers have dwindled, but we continue to meet once a month to support each other in what Mary Oliver has called "the season of snow." I am very grateful to my Houston friends who adopted me so willingly: Ruth Brodsky, Jean Goldberg, Pat Kaufman, and Iris Siegel—who can't see us or remember our other seasons, but still knows who we are by our voices.

I am still in shock over the sudden loss of my friend Bette Freundlich. We called each other every Sunday night to rehash the events of our favorite "soaps." Two other friends have enriched my life in significant ways: Phil's sister, Helen Simkin, is the Swiss Army Knife of friendship––I call on her for everything, and she always comes through. My other special friend is Linda Friedman. She shares my interests in art, culture, politics, why people do the things they do, and much more. She had the nerve to move to Austin a few years ago. We are always planning to see each other in one place or another and once in a while, we do.

Epiphany #6: I have tried to play all my family roles to the hilt, but my favorite role is my current one: Gran. I had just about given up hope that I would ever get this part when it finally happened. To my great surprise and pleasure, my children finally came through, and I am now playing grandmother of a splendid cast of three: Alexis (daughter of Lori and Jon), and Nathan and Elliot (sons of Jane and Michael). Although I am not really her grandmother, I consider myself something akin to it to Rebecca, Rick and Linda's daughter.

I am not the grandmother Bobo was. Life has changed. There is no iceman to carry fifty-pound chunks of ice into the wooden icebox in the back hall, and the coal man doesn't dump his coal on the basement floor.

My three grandchildren are growing up in a much bigger world than I did. They all have computers, and they have been to Europe more than once. They are accomplished athletes, singers, actors, dancers, writers, and artists. Despite their sophistication, I am happy to say they still have a strong sense of family. They are eager to know all the stories about their grandparents, their great-grandparents, and their great-greats.

Of course, their most avid interest is in hearing stories about the mischief their parents and their aunts and uncles got into when they were growing up. Vladimir Nabokov said telling these stories is a chance to reflect the ordinary "in the kindly mirrors of future times." I take a different view.

As a grandmother, isn't it my job to tell them about all the rotten pranks their parents pulled? As Hillel didn't exactly say, "If not me, who?" So, I have told them about the time Jane ran away from home, taking only her pimple medication and thirty-nine cents. And I have mentioned the elaborate Rube Goldberg contraptions Jon rigged up to keep us all out of his room when he was gone. I threw in the misdeeds of their Aunt Ashely, who discovered she could go AWOL after bedtime when we lived in the Pineacre house by taking the screen off her bedroom window, crawling onto the garage roof, and dropping six feet to the backyard.

I feel it's only fair to tell them these stories because I am certain their parents have told them about the rotten things we did to *them*. This narration was sure to include the compulsory dancing classes at the Outing Club, where they had to wear white gloves, dance with creeps of the opposite sex, and learn to curtsy and bow.

While I often speculate on my grandchildren's futures, which I may not live long enough to see, it gives me great pleasure to observe in them, now and then, a familiar expression or a character trait I recognize from a past generation. I see this as a symbol of perpetuity. Who knows? Perhaps a future generation will produce a little boy who wants to be a rabbi and specialize in exorcisms, or a little girl may materialize with an entrepreneurial spirit and peculiar toes, unable to resist the urge to cover her furniture with plastic sheets.

I have been privileged to share my life with five generations of my family. As with all lives, mine has not been perfect. I have had my share of disappointments and sorrow, but through the rough times and in my happiest moments, I could always feel the support of my family. They did not always approve, but they were there. That is what I hope gets passed along to each of the future generations I will never know.

The entire immigrant generation of our family is now gone. In writing this book, I hoped to bring them to life for those who never knew them. Unexpectedly—such was their vigor and brio—they would not stay on the page. As I wrote about them, they continued to argue, interrupting my thoughts, demanding to be heard. I have given them their chance to be heard in these stories. It's my turn to say, unequivocally, "This is the way it happened."

Afterword

Most people write a book and move on, but I can never leave well enough alone. Just as I reached the point in this book where I could see the light at the end of the tunnel, it occurred to me to turn around and include some family recipes. Recipes to me are mysteriously osmotic—artifacts still imbued with the spirit of the loved one who made these dishes for me.

I wanted to trap that power here, so I began to collect recipes from my cousins, my siblings, and my children. It was my goal to include at least one recipe from each branch of the family. This happened. Gathered here are recipes culled from our immigrant generation, some of which may have been recalled from their days in the shtetl, along with the signature dishes of the generations that followed. There are a few recipes from special friends who are like family. When a recipe came with comments, I tried to include them. For the ones without comments, I sometimes added my own thoughts.

Some of these recipes are appropriate to particular Jewish holidays. What could be more perfect than passing on traditional dishes to future generations to enjoy together on Jewish holidays? When I was a child, that was what I thought being Jewish meant: sitting around a dining room table in one house or another eating Jewish food with the rest of the family. I think this must be a common conclusion. As Alan King famously noted, "A short summary of every Jewish holiday: They tried to kill us. We won. Let's eat."

I didn't realize back then that we were passing along our traditions with those dinners. Is Judaism the only religion that feeds the body in the hope of reaching the soul? Not that Judaism is an intemperate, hedonistic religion. We have a lot of rules about what we eat, and I don't mean the 248 biblical—or rabbinical—rules dealing with food, which most of us don't observe, or even know about. I'm talking about the permutations the average Jew considers sacred.

We are unabashed snobs about how food should be prepared, and we are dictatorial about what goes with it. For example, I remember a distant relative by marriage who once put mayonnaise on her corned beef sandwich. No one ever got over that. She was referred to as "Mayonnaise" from then on. To illustrate this point, Milton Berle quipped: "Any time a person goes into a delicatessen and orders a pastrami on white bread, somewhere a Jew dies."

Recipes have been described as powerful talismans. Just in case bequeathing them can convey a pinch of immortality, I am including some of my own here.

From Our Various Kitchens

APPETIZERS

Gravlax (or Gravlox)

Ingredients

salmon fillets, scales removed
kosher salt
smidge of sugar
cracked peppercorns
liquid smoke
chopped dill, optional

Start with clean dry salmon. Rub salt, pepper, and dill (if using) on topside only. Cover thoroughly with plastic wrap and enclose in a plastic bag. Refrigerate for 36 hours, then remove salt with cold running water and dry with toweling. Using a pastry brush or your fingers, apply 1½ to 2½ tablespoons of liquid smoke. Wrap salmon in fresh plastic wrap and place in a fresh plastic bag. Refrigerate for 24 hours. Unwrap. Keep in refrigerator for easy slicing. (Keep your knife angled sharply when slicing. You can freeze the remaining salmon.)

Harry Schulman

I never make this without thinking of Uncle Harry. Even after we were old enough to drop the "Uncle," none of us did. This is the first recipe he passed along to all of us. There are easier recipes for this, but I always make this one.

Make-Ahead Hors d'Oeuvres

Ingredients

1 pkg Pillsbury Crescent Rolls
1 box Pillsbury mashed potatoes
1 can French-fried onions

Open the package of rolls and connect them, making one long roll. Cook the potatoes. Break the canned onions into small chunks and mix with the potatoes. Layer this mixture over the roll. Roll up and pinch the ends. Put the uncovered roll in the freezer to harden. When hard, slice the roll into servings and put on a cookie sheet. Bake for 30 minutes in a 375° oven.

Lillian Katz

Faux Chopped Liver
Ingredients
1 medium can peas, drained
1 medium onion, sliced
3 hard-boiled eggs
¾ cup walnuts
salt and pepper, to taste

Sauté the onion. Put all the other ingredients in the sauté pan and mix well. Place the mixture in a bowl and refrigerate. When cool, pulse in a processor until smooth. Better the next day.

Ann Schulman

Ann, without an "e" at the end, was Harry's wife. My mother spelled her own name "Anne." This could have been confusing, but we solved this problem by calling one "Big Ann" and the other "Little Anne" (sort of like the Edie Bouvier Beales of Grey Gardens). Since these designations were based on inches, not pounds, nobody was offended—particularly my mother, who eventually weighed more than Harry's Ann.

Helen's Heavenly Herring
Ingredients
1 large jar herring in wine sauce (not sour cream)
2 T regular mayonnaise (not light)
2 T sour cream
1 bunch of green onions
dash of celery seed

Drain herring well. Throw away all the onions and other seasonings that were in the jar with the herring. Cut up (or mince) the green onion, using both the white and the green parts. Add the mayonnaise and the sour cream (start with two tablespoons of each, add more to taste). Add celery seed to taste. Mix well. Serve on wheat crackers, cocktail rye bread, or crackers of your choice.

Helen Simkin

Helen, Phil's sister, is a special family friend who supplies us with this appetizer every Thanksgiving—it is her specialty. We have been known to stand at the kitchen counter and eat this for breakfast. The first time she made this for us, she sent along a note that said, "Although few people know it, one of the Pilgrims was Jewish—and herring was served on that first Thanksgiving, so enjoy!"

BRUNCH

Touch of Mexico Eggs

Ingredients

2 4-oz cans of Old El Paso whole green chiles
¾ pound shredded Monterey Jack cheese
4 eggs
nonstick cooking spray

Heat oven to 300°. Spray a 9" pie pan with cooking spray. Rinse, seed, and drain chiles. Line the bottom and sides of the pie pan with the chiles. Cover with cheese. Beat the eggs and carefully pour over cheese. Cook 1 hour.

Jane Stein

This simple, delicious recipe from my daughter, Jane, never fails. I don't do brunches any more, so I serve this as an appetizer. Unfortunately, my guests always seem to ask me for the recipe—then I have to admit how easy it is.

Blintz Casserole

Ingredients

½ stick margarine or butter
4 eggs
½ pint sour cream
¼ cup sugar
¼ t vanilla
1 T orange juice
10 frozen blintzes (1 pkg, either fruit or cheese)
dash of cinnamon, to taste

Mix eggs, sour cream, sugar, vanilla, and orange juice in a mixer. Melt margarine or butter in an 8" by 8" pan. Arrange blintzes in two rows and pour the sauce over them. Sprinkle cinnamon on top and bake in a 350° oven for 35–45 minutes, or until lightly browned. Serve with sour cream and jelly.

Diane Blas

Diane was my cousin, Aunt Lil's oldest daughter and my biggest rival for Bob's attention when we were growing up. She was the one who inherited Aunt Lil's long legs, and she had a great sense of style to go with them. She married, had four interesting daughters, and was later divorced. She died young—many years before Aunt Lil did. I wanted her to be represented in this book; I was told she made this recipe often.

French Toast Casserole

Ingredients

1 French bread (13—15 oz)
8 large eggs
2 cups half & half
1 cup milk
2 T granulated sugar
1 t vanilla extract
¼ t ground cinnamon
¼ t ground nutmeg
dash salt
praline topping (recipe follows)
maple syrup (optional)

Slice or cube bread (20 slices—but if you want to serve more people, cube the bread). Arrange bread in a generously buttered 9" by 13" dish in two rows, overlapping the slices. In a large bowl combine eggs, half & half, milk, sugar, vanilla, cinnamon, nutmeg, and salt. Beat with rotary beater or whisk until blended. Pour over bread, making sure everything is covered evenly with the milk and egg mixture. Cover with foil and refrigerate overnight. Cover with praline topping the next day.

Ingredients for praline topping

2 sticks butter
1 cup packed light brown sugar
1 cup chopped pecans
2 T light corn syrup
½ T ground cinnamon
½ teaspoon ground nutmeg

Preheat oven to 350°. Combine all ingredients and blend. Spread topping evenly over the bread and bake for 40 minutes, until puffed and lightly golden. Serve with maple syrup if desired.

Linda Schulman

Linda went on a cruise and this was served for brunch. She managed to wrangle the recipe from the captain and made the mistake of making this for us a few Thanksgivings ago. Now she's stuck with making it every year. It's a big recipe, but we manage to do away with it by the end of the holiday. It warms up well.

SALADS

Ambrosia

Ingredients

1 qt sour cream
2 cans cut-up pineapple
¾ lb marshmallows
¼ lb coconut

Combine all ingredients and chill. Serves 25.
Edna Siegel

Edna wasn't a Schulman, but she was my favorite Siegel, and this happens to be a very good recipe when you are having a party. You can add seedless grapes and berries of any kind.

Mandarin Orange Salad

Ingredients

4 T canned mandarin oranges, drained
2 T wine vinegar
2 T sugar
1 small pkg of sliced almonds, toasted
3 or 4 green onions, sliced (use green and white parts)
1 can of hearts of palm
1 can plain (not marinated) artichokes
¼ to ½ c salad oil
1 pkg of red leaf lettuce or romaine

Bring oranges, vinegar, and sugar to a slow boil in a small saucepan, simmer until syrupy. Cool. Add salad oil. To serve, add the other ingredients and toss. Serves six to eight.

Debbie Krasne

Cranberry Jell-O Mold

Ingredients

1 6-oz box cherry Jell-O
1½ cups boiling water
2 cans whole cranberry sauce,
2 cans mandarin oranges, drained
1 tart apple, diced
1 cup pecan pieces

Dissolve Jell-O in water, add ingredients in order. Refrigerate. Serves eight.

Lori Siegel

Can't-Miss-on-This-One Salad

Ingredients

3 large garlic cloves, minced
¼ t dry mustard
¼ t salt
½ t pepper
1 T lemon juice, fresh
1½ T grated Parmesan cheese
½ cup salad oil (or ¼ cup salad oil and ¼ cup olive oil)
2 pkgs mixed greens
top with tomato wedges, carrots, hard-boiled eggs, croutons, etc.

Combine garlic, mustard, salt and pepper, lemon juice, Parmesan cheese, and oil. Arrange greens and toppings in serving bowl. Shake dressing and pour over salad. Toss. Serves eight to ten.

Donna Siegel

Tomato Mozzarella Salad

Ingredients

2–3 ripe tomatoes, sliced thickly
¼ lb thinly sliced mozzarella
1 can flat anchovies
2 cloves garlic, minced
3 T chopped fresh basil
1 orange, peeled and segmented
wine vinegar, olive oil, freshly ground pepper to taste

Alternate the tomatoes and cheese slices on four plates. Lay the anchovies and orange segments over the tomatoes. Add garlic and basil on top. Drizzle vinegar and oil over all. Season with pepper.

Lois Landa

Lois and I met as freshmen at the University of Iowa. She was from Sioux City, so we knew some of the same people. We managed to stay in touch all the years I lived in Davenport, and when I moved to Houston we picked right up where we left off. Lois was a wonderful cook, but it didn't stop there: she was all about presentation. Her dishes were *finished*, with sprigs, blossoms, or something else she saw somewhere. It can truly be said that she lived her life with flair. She died recently after a long illness, but she left me with many fun memories and a few unusual *tchotchskies.* (This word is spelled many ways. I decided to italicize it here even though it appears occasionally in the *New York Times*. No matter how it's spelled, it always means a trinket or knickknack of inconsequential value.)

Baby Blue Salad

Ingredients

for the salad:

1 4-oz package of blue cheese, crumbled
2 oranges, peeled and sliced thin
¾ pound mixed greens
1 pint fresh strawberries, quartered
balsamic vinaigrette (recipe follows)
sweet and spicy pecans (recipe follows)

Place the mixed greens and blue cheese in a bowl. Reserve the oranges and strawberries for garnish. Prepare the balsamic vinaigrette.

balsamic vinaigrette:

½ cup balsamic vinegar
3 T Dijon mustard
3 T honey
2 garlic cloves, minced
2 small shallots, minced
¼ teaspoon salt, ¼ teaspoon pepper
1 cup olive oil

Whisk together all but the olive oil. Gradually whisk in the oil. Prepare the pecans.

sweet and spicy pecans:

¼ cup sugar and 2 tablespoons more
1 teaspoon chili powder
dash of ground red pepper
1 cup warm water

Stir ¼ cup sugar and the warm water until sugar dissolves. Add pecans, soak 10 minutes. Drain. Discard syrup. Combine 2 T of sugar, chili powder, and red pepper. Add pecans. Toss to

coat. Place nuts on greased baking sheet. Bake at 350° for 10 minutes, stirring once.
Assemble salad: Toss mixed greens with vinaigrette and blue cheese. Place on 6 plates. Arrange orange slices over the greens. Sprinkle strawberries. Top with pecans.

Vicki Gammill

My sister's lovely summer salad. It's a bit of a stretch for those of us who usually cook with four ingredients, but it's a treat for your taste buds: sweet, sour, salt, and hot—all at once. And with hunks of good bread and a nice glass of wine, it's dinner.

FRUIT AND VEGETABLE DISHES

Sweet Potato Mold
Ingredients
4–6 large sweet potatoes
2 eggs
1 cup light brown sugar
1½ –2 sticks of butter or margarine
1 cup chopped walnuts or pecans

Peel potatoes. Cut, boil, and drain. Add ¾ stick of butter and eggs. Mash potatoes, eggs, brown sugar, and butter together in a mixer. Grease a metal mold (or a Bundt pan). Place chopped nuts on the bottom of the mold. Mix the remaining softened butter with the brown sugar and cover the nuts. Pack the potato mixture into the mold. Place the mold in a large roasting pan with enough water to cover the bottom so the nuts, butter and sugar are covered. When the water boils, the sugar and butter melt to form a wonderful glaze. Partially cool (10 minutes). Very carefully remove the mold, using a spatula to cut around the edges. Use a large enough platter, with some depth, so that the glaze can ooze out over the mold when you turn it over. It will come out easily with the glaze and nuts on top, looking good and tasting delicious.

Lillian Katz

Aunt Lil could never tell us how many people her recipes served. Maybe it was because no matter how much she made, and no matter how many eaters, nothing was ever left.

Scalloped Pineapple
Ingredients
2 large cans crushed pineapple
1 cup brown sugar
1 cup white sugar
1 T lemon juice
7 slices white bread, crusts removed and torn into pieces
Rice Krispies, crushed
butter

Combine all the ingredients except the Rice Krispies in a casserole. Cover with crushed Rice Krispies and dot with butter. Bake 45 minutes in a 350° oven. Serves 10-12.

Lori Siegel

This is a must for Thanksgiving. Even the kids like it.

Sautéed Cauliflower
Ingredients
1 whole cauliflower, cored and boiled
1 beaten egg
seasoned bread crumbs to cover florets
cooking oil to cover bottom of the pan

Break cauliflower into florets. Dredge in beaten egg, then in seasoned breadcrumbs. Sauté in hot oil until crisp and starting to brown. Serves four to six.

Ann Schulman

Spinach Casserole

Ingredients

2 10-oz pkgs frozen chopped spinach
1 14-oz can artichoke hearts packed in water, drained
1¼ sticks of butter, divided
1 8-oz pkg cream cheese, softened
1 8-oz can water chestnuts, sliced
dash garlic salt, optional
½ cup fresh bread crumbs

Cook the spinach and drain. Cut artichoke hearts in half. Line a greased 8" by 12" baking dish with artichoke hearts. Melt one stick butter in a large saucepan. Add cream cheese, spinach, water chestnuts, and garlic salt (if using). Cover the artichoke hearts with this mixture. Sprinkle with breadcrumbs, pat with remaining butter. Bake at 400° for 20–25 minutes. Serves 8.

Donna Siegel

Corn Casserole

Ingredients

1 stick butter
1 14-oz can whole kernel corn, drained
1 14-oz can cream-style corn
1 8-oz pkg sour cream
2 eggs
1 box Jiffy Corn Muffin Mix
¼ cup of sugar

Melt butter. Add drained corn and cream-style corn. Beat eggs with sour cream and sugar. Blend into corn mixture. Add muffin mix and stir. Bake 45 minutes at 350° or until top gets golden brown.

Ann Schulman

STARCHES

Kraut Noodles

Ingredients

1 pkg of wide, no-yolk egg noodles
½ head cabbage, cut into thin strips
1 onion, cut into thin strips
glob of butter (can mix with olive oil)

In a large saucepan, cook the noodles as directed on the package. Put the butter in a pan big enough to cook the cabbage and the onion more or less to death—until they are browned and wrinkly. Mix in the noodles and even MORE butter. Only two words to describe this dish: AWE SOME! This was my mother-in-law, Laura Stein's classic dish, and now it is mine.

Jane Stein

Prize-Winning Kugel Supreme

Ingredients

½ pound medium noodles
¾ stick butter
1 cup milk
1 cup apricot juice
1 4-oz pkg cream cheese
½ cup of sugar
1 t vanilla
3 eggs
nonstick cooking spray
topping: ½ 7-oz box of corn flakes, ¼ cup sugar, 1 t cinnamon, ¾ stick softened butter

Spray glass 8" by 10" pan with non-stick spray. Cut butter into small pieces. Scatter in pan. Spread noodles over the butter*. In a food processor, mix cream cheese and sugar until creamy. Place in a large bowl. Beat in eggs, milk, apricot juice, and vanilla. Pour mixture over noodles and cover them all, even if you have to break up the noodles.
Make topping as follows: Place the corn flakes in a bowl, add sugar and cinnamon and mix. Using your hands, soften the butter and add to the corn flake combination, mixing well. Crush the flakes until they crumble to the size of peas. Scatter the mixture on top of the noodles. Be sure all the noodles are covered. Bake at 350° for 45 minutes. The kugel is done when the center is solid.

Nancy Schulman

*Nancy says you can cook the noodles first or let them cook in the sauce. She entered this recipe in a local cooking contest and won first place. Her husband, Dennis, says it's always a hit.

Crown Noodle Pudding

Ingredients

1 stick margarine, divided
¾ cup brown sugar
1 cup chopped walnuts
1 16-oz package of medium noodles
1 t salt
4 beaten eggs
¾ cup applesauce
½ t cinnamon
½ to 1 cup sugar to taste
nonstick cooking spray

Cook and drain noodles. Spray Bundt pan with nonstick cooking spray. Pour melted margarine into pan. Place brown sugar over the margarine, top with chopped nuts. In a large bowl, mix remaining ingredients, add noodles and mix again. Pour carefully over the nuts and brown sugar in the pan. Bake at 350° until brown, about an hour. Loosen the edges with a knife. Cover with a serving dish. Turn noodle pudding upside down on the plate to serve.

Lillian Katz

Quick and Easy Farfel

Ingredients

2 to 3 T margarine
1 8-oz pkg farfel
1 envelope dry onion soup mix
1 t soy sauce
1 4-oz can mushrooms
2 cups boiling water
margarine

Melt margarine in a heavy 12" frying pan. Add uncooked farfel and sprinkle with the remaining ingredients. Brown over high heat. Pour 2 cups of boiling water over the mixture. Cover and cook on low heat until the liquid is absorbed. Makes 6–8 servings.

Sheilah Schiff

Sheilah was Aunt Lil's youngest daughter, who died too soon. She was an amazing woman, a wonderful hostess, and a world-class shopper. She specialized in TJ Maxx. To those she left behind, that will always be Sheilah's store.

Oyster Stuffing

Ingredients for cornbread

1 cup self-rising cornmeal
½ cup self-rising flour
¾ cup buttermilk
2 eggs
2 T vegetable oil

Preheat oven to 350º. Combine all the ingredients and pour into a greased shallow baking dish. Bake for 20 to 25 minutes. Remove from the oven and let cool.

Ingredients for stuffing

cooled cornbread (see above)
7 slices white bread, dried in warm oven
1 sleeve saltine crackers
2 cups chopped celery
1 large chopped onion
8 T butter
1 cup chicken stock
1 t salt
½ t freshly ground black pepper
1 t dried sage
1 T poultry seasoning
5 eggs, beaten
2 pints oysters, drained

Crumble the bread slices, cornbread, and crackers. Mix together and set aside. Sauté chopped celery and onion in butter until transparent, about 5 to 10 minutes. Pour over the bread mixture. Add stock. Mix well. Add salt, pepper, sage, and poultry seasoning. Mix. Add beaten eggs and mix. Add oysters and mix. Pour into a greased pan. Bake at 350° for 45 minutes.

Vicki Gammill

My sister, Vicki, is always given the stuffing responsibility for Thanksgiving. It's a formidable task, because the stuffing is far more significant to us than the turkey. After many years of experimentation followed by a lot of commotion and raucous voting, this has become our Thanksgiving favorite. Still, we haven't tasted Helen Baker's recipe, which follows. There could be a turkey stuffing bake-off sometime in the future. Vicki's husband, Larry Gammill, is a great cook, and he makes the gravy. It is not included here because he is the only one who knows how to make it from scratch—without a package—and he doesn't follow a recipe.

Bread Stuffing

Ingredients

2 loaves challah
Swanson's chicken broth (not salt-free, not organic)
2 chopped onions
5 chopped stalks of celery
1 chopped green bell pepper
1 chopped red bell pepper
6 eggs, beaten
2 cans drained mushrooms (stems and pieces are fine)
1 T rubbed sage
extra turkey parts, thighs and legs are best
garlic salt
Lawry's seasoning to taste
cooking oil

Pull apart the challah, place in a large bowl, and nearly cover it with the chicken broth. Let the bread soak up as much broth as it can. Don't squeeze. In a very large skillet, brown the onions, celery, and peppers in cooking oil. Drain excess broth from the bread. Add the bread to the vegetables and cook over medium high heat, turning often until bread is brown. Transfer to a large bowl, add eggs, mushrooms, spices, and the seasoning. Put the dressing in a roaster or large pan, top with turkey thighs and legs. Cover and bake in a 325° oven until the top is brown and the inside is sticky but not wet—about 2 to 3 hours. You can remove the cover for additional browning.

Helen Baker

Aunt Helen was the oldest sister, and she—more than the others—cooked by the way things looked and tasted. I'm not sure she ever followed a recipe, but she was a good, right-brained cook. As Helen's daughter, Debbie Krasne, points out, this recipe comes from the kitchen of a woman who never owned a measuring cup or a spoon! Unencumbered by such trivia, this is the recipe that has come to mean Thanksgiving to her family, which now includes Helen's great grandchildren. Debbie roasts a whole turkey separately.

ENTRÉES

Grilled Swordfish
Ingredients
swordfish fillets
garlic salt
ground fresh pepper
margarine

Mash the garlic salt and ground pepper into fish on both sides with the back of a spoon, then slather margarine on both sides. Broil fish on lowest rack setting for 8½–9 minutes depending on the thickness of the fish, turn, and broil about the same time on the other side.

Paul Schulman
Paul/Rick says, "I cook everything this way—salmon, Dungeness crab. What doesn't taste good cooked with garlic and butter? And having one recipe cuts down on my confusion."

Our Clambake Legacy

Ingredients

small red potatoes
whole onions
chicken breasts and legs (boiled chicken is bland, so season heavily as desired)
corn on the cob, can be fresh or frozen
steamer clams, cleaned with brush (if you can't find clams, use mussels)
water for steaming, about 2 or 3 inches
2–3 bottles of clam broth for extra flavor
enough lobster to feed your crowd

A steamer pot with a spigot on the lower section is best, because you can pour the infused clam broth into cups for dipping and drinking, and the holes at the bottom allow the steam to rise. If you don't have a steamer pot, improvise something to keep the food out of the water while it is steaming. Start heating the water while you fill the upper section with all the listed ingredients. When the lobster is bright red, you are finished—usually about 30–40 minutes from the time the water starts steaming. All the clams or mussels should be open. Throw away the unopened ones.

George Schulman

Dad was famous for his clambakes. We held an annual clambake for friends and family during our reunions in Davenport. He ordered the lobsters and steamers from Damariscotta, Maine. The tables in our backyard were filled with happily munching guests and buttery chins.

Crusty Tuna Trio

Ingredients

2 cans tuna in oil, 6 ½ –7 oz each
1½ cups soft bread cubes
¼ cup chopped onion
½ cup mayonnaise
1 t lemon juice
½ cup evaporated milk
salt and pepper to taste
corn flake crumbs

Drain oil from tuna into a mixing bowl. Add bread cubes to the oil and blend. Mix in onion, salt, pepper, mayonnaise, and lemon juice. Flake tuna and add. For appetizers, shape mixture into 1 oz balls; for croquettes, shape into ovals; for loaf, shape into a loaf pan. Dip in evaporated milk and sprinkle with crumbs. Place on a foil-lined baking sheet. Bake in a 375º oven: 10 minutes for balls, 20 minutes for croquettes, 30 minutes shaped in a loaf pan. Makes
5 dozen balls, 6 croquettes, or one loaf.

Elsie Babbitt

Cabbage Rolls

Ingredients

1 head cabbage
1–2 pounds ground beef (or ground turkey)
1 onion, chopped
1 can jellied cranberry sauce
1 jar chili sauce
3–4 ground crackers
1–2 eggs, beaten
small amount of water
salt and pepper
nonstick cooking spray

In a bowl, combine meat, onion, crackers, water, salt, and pepper. Form meatballs. Immerse the cabbage in boiling water for a few minutes to soften. Remove the cabbage, cut out the core, and pull off the big leaves carefully, leaving them whole if possible. Spray a large oven dish with nonstick cooking spray. Sliver the smaller pieces of the cabbage and place in the bottom of the dish. Roll the meatballs in the cabbage leaves, tucking in the sides of the leaves, and turn them seam-side down in the dish—no need to skewer with toothpicks. Mix the cranberry sauce and the chili sauce together and pour over the top. Cover with foil and place in a 325°–350° oven for 2 hours or longer.

Donna Siegel

Standing Rib Roast

Ingredients

6–8 pound rib roast
butter, softened
garlic
onion
thyme
salt and pepper

Preheat oven to 325°. Combine butter and seasonings into a paste. Stand roast on a rack in a large roasting pan, fatty side up. Brush paste generously over the top and sides of the roast. Form a loose foil tent over the roast. Bake about 20–25 minutes per pound for medium rare. Let rest for 20–30 minutes before carving.

Anne Schulman

We don't remember Mother using a thermometer or doing anything special, but her roasts were always perfect—medium rare and delicious. What we can all remember is how the house smelled when we walked through the back door into the kitchen after our golf game. If you use a meat thermometer, figure 130° to 135° for medium rare.

New Orleans Barbeque Shrimp

Ingredients

2 sticks salted butter
1 cup vegetable oil
1 t chopped garlic
1 t lemon juice
4 bay leaves, crushed
¾ t pepper
2 t Italian seasoning
1 T paprika
½ t each: basil, cayenne, oregano, salt
2 pounds of the largest shrimp you can find, still in the shell

Melt butter in a Dutch oven. Add remaining ingredients except shrimp. Stir over medium heat until the sauce boils. Reduce heat to low and simmer 8 minutes, stirring frequently. Remove Dutch oven from heat for at least 30 minutes. About 20 minutes before serving, add shrimp. Mix thoroughly. Cook over medium heat for 6–8 minutes, until shrimp turn pink. Finish in a preheated 450° oven for 10 minutes. Ladle shrimp and sauce in 4 to 6 bowls and serve with crusty French bread. This is a messy dish because you will be peeling off the shrimp shells at the table. You'll need a "graveyard" for the shells and plenty of napkins. Add a salad— and pretend you are at Pascal Manale's in New Orleans.

Donna Siegel

Gedempte (Braised) Chicken

Ingredients

2 large onions, sliced
3½–4 pounds chicken, cut into 8 pieces
1 T paprika
1 t salt
½ t pepper
¼ cup of water

Preheat oven to 325°. In a heavy Dutch oven, spread half the onions on the bottom of the pot and add water. Season the chicken with paprika, salt, and pepper. Place in the pot and cover with the remaining onions. Cover the pot tightly. Bake 1½ hours.

Anne Schulman

Sauerbraten

Ingredients

¾ cup red wine vinegar
¾ cup dry red wine
1 medium carrot, sliced thin
1 medium onion, sliced thin
¼ cup sugar
5 peppercorns
2 cloves
1 bay leaf
3 T vegetable oil
1 T flour
chopped parsley
4 pound boneless beef roast, bottom or top round
2 cups of water
butter clumps

In a medium-sized saucepan, simmer vinegar, wine, carrot, onion, sugar, peppercorns, cloves, and bay leaf in 2 cups of water for 15 minutes. Cool to room temperature. Put meat in a bowl and pour sauce over meat. Cover and refrigerate for 2–3 days, turning meat a couple of times a day. Take meat out of marinade, but reserve marinade. Put meat in a large pot or Dutch oven with a lid. Strain the marinade into a measuring cup. You should have around 2 cups (add water if necessary). Pour the strained liquid over meat and cover the pot tightly. Bake around 3 hours.

For gravy: while meat is resting, pour the juices into a saucepan and bring to a boil. Whisk in flour and butter clumps in small pieces. Simmer the sauce for a couple of minutes. Slice the meat across the grain and spoon sauce over each slice. Sprinkle with parsley. Another Laura Stein production. Yummy.

Jane Stein

Sweet and Sour Meatballs

Ingredients

2 pounds of ground beef
2 eggs
2 T bread crumbs
½ cup of water
1 t of salt

Mix all the ingredients and form balls. Drop the meatballs into boiling water for 10 minutes. Strain until the meatballs are free of fat and water.

For the sauce:

2 cups of water
½ can whole cranberry sauce
2 T grape jelly
½ T lemon juice
2 T sugar

Mix the sauce ingredients and put in a large saucepan. Bring to a boil, add meatballs, and cook for an hour. This recipe can be frozen in a plastic zip bag until needed.

Audrey Remer

Audrey, Lillian's only living daughter, brought her mother to live with her for the last few years of Aunt Lil's life. It was a wonderful time for both of them. They became closer than they had even been. It was the best gift they could have given each other. Audrey was a big help to me with the details of Aunt Lil's recipes, and she graciously passed along some good ones of her own. Thanks, Audrey.

Company Brisket

Ingredients

1½" piece fresh ginger, peeled and cut into thin strips
2 cups dry red wine
1½ t coarse salt
1 T Dijon mustard
4 cloves garlic, peeled and crushed with flat of knife
2 bay leaves
3 T dark brown sugar
¼ cup apple cider vinegar
6 pound beef brisket or chuck roast
3 T canola oil
½ t freshly ground black pepper
¼ t ground allspice
2 large yellow onions, thinly sliced
1 14½-oz reduced-sodium beef broth
16 large pitted prunes (1 cup)
18 dried apricots (1 cup)
¼ cup brandy
1 cup water

In a large plastic bag that can be resealed, place ginger, wine, 1 teaspoon salt, mustard, garlic, bay leaves, brown sugar, and vinegar. Shake to combine. Add brisket and seal carefully. Refrigerate overnight, turning several times to coat the meat. Preheat oven to 325°. Remove meat from bag (reserving marinade) and pat dry. In a large ovenproof casserole with a tightly fitting lid, heat oil over medium-high heat. Sprinkle meat with remaining salt, pepper, and allspice. Brown on all sides, about 8 minutes. Add onions, reserved marinade, and broth. Cover and cook 1 hour.

Meanwhile, in a small saucepan combine prunes, apricots, brandy, and water. Bring to a boil. Remove from heat, cover and let stand for 10 minutes. Drain, discarding soaking liquid, reserving prunes and apricots. Add prunes and apricots to the casserole and cook 1–1½ hours or even longer, until meat is very tender. Remove meat to serving platter and cover to keep warm. Skim fat from surface of casserole and bring to a simmer. Cook 5 minutes, until sauce is reduced. Slice meat and arrange prunes, apricots, and onions around the slices. Ladle sauce over meat, pour remaining sauce in a gravy boat and serve.

Sue Fine

Sue Fine, Elsie Babbitt's daughter, says, "If you put ten Jews together, you'll get ten different recipes for brisket. This one is fancier than most, but I omit the prunes and apricots when preparing it for my grandchildren and certain other family members who don't know what's *really* good!"

DESSERTS

Bananas Foster

Ingredients

6 under-ripe bananas, sliced lengthwise
¾ stick butter
1 cup brown sugar
1 T cinnamon
¼ cup rum

Melt the butter with brown sugar and cinnamon in a skillet. Add sliced bananas and sauté in sugar mixture until bananas are glazed. Pour in rum and flame. Serve with vanilla ice cream or whipped cream.

Ron Schulman

I'm not sure how Sunday morning brunch at Brennan's got added to our "Mandatory List of Gustatory Indulgencies" when we visited our parents in New Orleans. I suspect that Ron and Rick were the perps on this one, because they loved bananas foster. When our parents moved from New Orleans, Ron was forced to learn how to make it. Now it is a special feature at Thanksgiving—after Vicki's dessert, the pumpkin pie, and the pecan pie are gone.

Hello Dollies!

Ingredients

1 stick of butter
2 cups graham cracker crumbs
1 cup chocolate chips
1 cup coconut flakes
1 cup chopped pecans
1 13-oz can condensed milk

Melt butter in 9" x 13" pan. Pat in cracker crumbs, add chocolate chips, coconut, and nuts in layers. Pour milk over all. Bake for 25 to 30 minutes in at 350°. Cool. Cut into bars or squares.

Ann Schulman

This is an old-fashioned dessert that you can't even find in most modern cookbooks. Why is this? Look at the ingredients! On the other hand, look how easily it all comes together. It's a toss-up.

Mandelbrot

Ingredients

1 cup sugar
½ cup oil
3 eggs
1 cup chopped nuts
½ cup chocolate chips
3 cups flour, sifted twice with 2 t baking powder

Mix sugar and oil. Add eggs one at a time, mixing each time. Add nuts and chocolate chips. Mix. Add the flour gradually. Knead dough until thoroughly mixed. Divide mixture into 4 parts. Dough will be sticky. Sprinkle a little flour on top of each part; roll out to 15" by 1½" wide (don't add any more flour, or it will get too heavy). Bake one sheet at a time at 350° for 20–25 minutes. Touch for firmness. Take out of the oven and cut into 1" slices. Turn pieces on their sides, replace in oven for 10 minutes until lightly brown. Repeat.

Elsie Babbitt

Mandelbrot

Ingredients

3 eggs
¾ cup oil
¾ cup sugar
2 t baking powder
2½ cups flour
¼ t salt
1 cup chopped almonds
1 t vanilla
mixture of sugar and cinnamon (optional)

Beat eggs and sugar together. Add oil and blend. Add baking powder, flour, and salt. Blend well to a soft dough. With floured hands, shape dough into 2 long loaves, about 2½"–3" wide and 1" high. Place on a cookie sheet that was sprayed with nonstick cooking spray. Bake at 350° for about 40 minutes or until lightly browned. Cool. Cut into 1"–1½" slices. If desired, sprinkle with a mixture of sugar and cinnamon. Turn off the oven and put the Mandelbrot back in the oven for about 20–30 minutes to toast. Keeps well.

Lillian Katz

This is not a competition of "The Dueling Mandelbrots"—just two delicious versions we have enjoyed for many years.

The "It-Wouldn't-Be-Thanksgiving-Without-It" Dessert

Ingredients

Crust

1 cup all-purpose flour
1 stick butter or margarine
1 cup whole pecans or walnuts

First layer

8 oz softened cream cheese
1 cup powered sugar
1 cup Cool Whip

Second layer

3 cups milk
1 small box chocolate instant pudding
1 small box vanilla instant pudding

Third layer

1 cup Cool Whip
Butterfinger or Twix chocolate candy bar

To make the crust, combine flour and butter; press nuts where you can in the dough. Press into a 9" by 13" pan. Bake at 350° for about 20 minutes (until lightly browned) and let cool. To make the first layer, combine cream cheese, powered sugar, and Cool Whip. Spread over crust. To make the second layer: combine milk and the chocolate and vanilla instant puddings. Mix until thickened. Spread over the first layer. To make the third layer, spread the rest of the Cool Whip over the top. Grate candy bar over the Cool Whip. Refrigerate at least 6 hours before serving. This dessert can be made ahead of time and frozen. Take it out of the freezer 12 hours before serving to thaw.

Vicki Gammill

Princess Cake (Chocolate Chip Coffee Cake)

Ingredients for the dough

2½ cups flour
2 T sugar
1 t salt
2 sticks butter or margarine, melted
¼ cup milk
3 eggs, separated
2 packages yeast
¼ cup warm water

Ingredients for the filling

1 cup sugar
3 egg whites
½ cup chopped nuts
½ cup chocolate chips
½ cup sugar and 2 teaspoons cinnamon, mixed
nonstick cooking spray

Mix yeast with ¼ cup of warm water and ½ teaspoon of sugar and let rise (follow recipe on the package). In a medium-sized bowl, mix the flour, the rest of the sugar, and salt and set aside. Add milk to the melted margarine or butter and set aside. Cover the egg whites and refrigerate. Beat the yolks slightly. Place the risen yeast mixture into the flour, sugar, and salt mixture; add the egg yolks, then the milk and melted margarine or butter mixture. Mix with a wooden spoon until the mixture forms a shiny ball and leaves the sides of the bowl clean. Cover snugly with foil and place in the refrigerator overnight or about 8 hours.

To make the filling: beat the 3 egg whites, gradually adding the cup of sugar until soft peaks form. Add the chopped nuts and chocolate chips and mix by hand. Sprinkle with cinnamon/ sugar mixture.

To bake: preheat oven to 325°. Spray a sponge cake pan with

nonstick spray. Roll half the dough into a 12" by 20" rectangle, spread half of the filling mixture over the top and roll like a jellyroll with the ends meeting. Place the roll in the pan with the seam on top. Do the same with the other half of the dough, placing the seam down on top of the first roll. With the point of a knife, make slits along the top about 2 inches apart. Cover with a clean dishtowel and place in a warm spot for 30 minutes. Then bake for an hour. Place on a rack to cool.

Elsie Babbitt

This is Aunt Elsie's very elegant signature dish. You can see why. She made it for very special occasions—and at the request of any of her visiting nieces and nephews. It won't be the same without her, but now we can make it any time we want.

Healthful Apple Crisp

Ingredients

6 cups peeled, sliced Gala apples (or equivalent)
½ t cinnamon or more, to taste
½ cup sugar, plus 2 tablespoons
5 T butter
¾ cup rolled oats
½ cup walnuts or pecans pieces

Heat oven to 375º. Toss apples with half the cinnamon and 2 tablespoons sugar. Spread in a lightly buttered 8"–9" baking pan. Combine remaining cinnamon and sugar in a food processor with butter, oats, and nuts. Pulse a few times, just until ingredients are combined. Spread topping over apples. Bake about 40 minutes, or until topping is brown and apples are tender. Serve warm, cold, or at room temperature. Servings: 6–8.

Donna Siegel

Prize-Winning Cheesecake Royale*

Ingredients for the crust

20 graham crackers
¼ cup butter, melted
2 T sugar

Ingredients for the Filling

2 eggs
½ cup sugar
12 oz cream cheese
½ t vanilla

Ingredients for the topping

1½ cup sour cream
2 T sugar
1 t vanilla

Mix the ingredients for the crust thoroughly. Place the mixture in the bottom of a pie pan and up to ½"–1" along the sides. Refrigerate until cool. Pour the filling over the cooled crust and bake in a 375° oven for 20 minutes. Cover the filling with the topping. Bake for 5 minutes in a 400° oven.
Audrey Remer

*This recipe won a citywide competition.

PASSOVER DISHES

Matzo Farfel Muffins

Ingredients

4 cups matzo farfel
4 cups boiling water
1 T butter or margarine
6 eggs
nonstick cooking spray

Pour boiling water over the farfel and cover for 10 minutes. Spray muffin pans with nonstick cooking spray and fill with farfel mix. Bake in a 400° oven for 35 minutes.
Options: before pouring the boiling water over the farfel, you can add sautéed onions and mushrooms—or cottage cheese, cinnamon, sugar, and vanilla to the mixture.

Lillian Katz

Charoset

Ingredients

2 apples, peeled, cored, and grated
1 cup finely chopped walnuts
1 T cinnamon
2 T sugar
1 T kosher sweet Passover wine

In a mixing bowl, blend all ingredients until smooth and well blended. Cover and refrigerate until ready to serve. Makes 2 cups.

Sheilah Shiff

Coconut Macaroons

Ingredients

1 14-oz bag shredded coconut
1 T vanilla
1 15-oz can condensed milk

Heat oven to 350°. Mix ingredients together, drop by spoonful on a greased cookie sheet and bake for 10–12 minutes. Cool on wire rack immediately.
Options: add 2 cups chopped walnuts or pecans to the mixture. For chocolate macaroons, drizzle with melted semisweet chocolate chips.

Lori Siegel

Matzo Farfel Bark

Ingredients

2 cups matzo farfel
raisins or nuts to taste
1 8-oz pkg of semisweet chocolate chips

Melt chocolate in the microwave. Combine with other ingredients. Spread on wax paper. Flatten with spatula. Refrigerate. Break off pieces to eat.

Elsie Babbitt

Chocolate Pecan Matzo

Ingredients

3½ sheets of matzo
½ cup butter, melted
½ cup brown sugar
1½ cups semisweet chocolate chips
chopped pecans to taste

Heat oven to 350°. Arrange the sheets of matzo on a parchment-lined baking sheet. Mix the melted butter with the brown sugar, stirring until the sugar is dissolved. Cook 5–10 minutes, until the mixture is thick. Spread over the matzo and bake in the oven for 5 minutes. Remove matzo from the oven and sprinkle with chocolate chips. Let stand for 5 minutes, then spread the chocolate over the matzo. Sprinkle with chopped pecans, pressing the nuts into the chocolate so they stick. Refrigerate and break into pieces.

Lori Siegel

Epilogue: My Obituary (Or, How to Make Sure You Get the Final Word)

"When I die, I want to die like my grandfather,
who died peacefully in his sleep.
Not screaming like all the passengers in his car."
—Author Unknown

I am like the entertainer who keeps reappearing for another encore, even if the audience isn't clapping. Call me a control freak, but I just couldn't leave the delicious task of writing my obituary to someone else. A memoir has been described as an arbitrary selection process by a very biased participant. What better reason could there be to complete the job and write my own obituary? Who is more biased in my favor than I am?

Although the pursuit of worldly goods may keep us busy throughout our lives, a trip to any nursing home will confirm that what turns out to be significant to us is a box of pictures and a lifetime of memories. That's what I am leaving behind—this book of memories and countless albums of photographs.

My only regret is that I didn't do more things in extremely bad taste. I know I would have enjoyed wantonness and depravity. I probably would have been very good at them too, but how many of us ever really live up to our potential? To those I leave behind, please don't read *A Woman of Valor, Worth More Than Rubies* at my funeral. This is how I would like to be remembered:

Donna Siegel, famed author and infamous libertine, collapsed and died shortly after her triumphant ascent to the top of Mount Kilimanjaro in Africa. She was 96, but she still looked good. As she requested, she was buried in a slinky teddy and high-heeled *nafke* shoes. (If you don't know the word, look it up.) Although she was told "you can't take it with you," she took her favorite possession, her iMac G5 computer with its 24-inch screen, just in case.

According to her family, she did not go quietly into the still, dark night. To the end, she was a pain in the neck, protesting that she wasn't ready to go because she still had a few body parts that were working. However, her family pointed out, *they* were ready. And besides, she already had the 3.5 statistically predicted chronic diseases for a woman her age: a yeast infection, an over-stimulated libido, a heart murmur synchronous with Dave Brubeck's "Take Five," and half a case of athlete's foot (her left one).

Ms. Siegel had a number of degrees from various institutions: a bachelor's degree in industrial photography, a master's degree in public health, and she was working on her doctorate in cultural anthropology. She was about to defend her dissertation entitled, "Beowulf and Snoop Dogg: Speaking in Indiscernible Tongues."

Even if she would have completed her PhD, it is doubtful that she would have pursued a career in that field, either. Ms. Siegel did not believe in *using* her degrees; she was only interested in taking classes and acquiring them. As anyone who knew her would confirm, she was the consummate lifelong learner. She was very proud of her AARP award, which she received in recognition for her ruthless pursuit of pointless information.

Nothing was too obscure for Ms. Siegel to research for hours on her iMac. She could spend an entire day checking on the best way to boil an egg. Due to her predilection for idle pursuit, she was recently commissioned by the Manischewitz Corporation to study the indigent populations of Litvak and Ashkenazi grape stompers.

During her long and tempestuous (some would say contemptuous) life, Ms. Siegel published a number of books on a variety of subjects. Her best-known work is *You Can Go Home Again, But Who Wants to?* She won the coveted Plotkin prize for her latest book, *How to Create and Raise a Dysfunctional Family.*

She leaves behind an exhausted family, many unusual friends, and a number of happy former and current lovers.

Acknowledgment

I began to think about finding a proofreader when I realized I couldn't think of anything else to add to my book. As fate would have it, I sat across the table from an interesting woman at my temple's book club meeting who mentioned she had been a proofreader for an architectural company. Since this book had reached architectural proportions by then, I asked her if she would be interested in taking on this project, and she agreed.

Little did I know how thorough she would be, how many little red marks would soon appear on each page of my manuscript, which began to look as though it had been invaded by a bad case of German measles.

It turned out that she knew Yiddish well enough to apply her red pencil to all my italicized words; she was a cook, demanding to know if the garlic referenced in a recipe was supposed to be minced, chopped, or crushed; and she was a lay cantor, knowledgeable about things like my grandfather's havdalah spice box, which I now know was passed around for everyone to smell, thus marking the end of the Sabbath.

Heartfelt thanks to Cyd Baron, my proofreader extraordinaire, who could have put this book to music. She also plays the guitar.